Zen *in the art of the* **SAT**

Other Graphia Titles

A Certain Slant of Light
by Laura Whitcomb

Open the Unusual Door: True Life Stories of
Adventure, Challenge, and Success by Black Americans
edited by Barbara Summers

I Can't Tell You
by Hillary Frank

Lost in the Labyrinth
by Patrice Kindl

Comfort
by Carolee Dean

I Just Hope It's Lethal: Poems of Sadness, Madness, and Joy
collected by Liz Rosenberg and Deena November

Dunk
by David Lubar

The Education of Robert Nifkin
by Daniel Pinkwater

Zen
in the art of the
SAT

How to Think, Focus, and Achieve Your Highest Score

MATT BARDIN *and* SUSAN FINE

G RAPHIA

AN IMPRINT OF HOUGHTON MIFFLIN COMPANY

BOSTON 2005

For information about permission to reproduce selections from this book, write to Permissions,
Houghton Mifflin Company, 215 Park Avenue South, New York, New York 10003.

www.houghtonmifflinbooks.com

The text of this book is set in 9.5-point Palatino.

SAT is the registered trademark of the College Board, which has not endorsed this publication.

Library of Congress Cataloging-in-Publication Data
Bardin, Matt.
Zen in the art of the SAT : how to think, focus, and achieve your highest score /
written by Matt Bardin and Susan Fine.
p. cm.
ISBN 0-618-57488-3 (pbk. : alk. paper)
1. Scholastic Assessment Test—Study guides. I. Fine, Susan. II. Title.
LB2353.57.B36 2005   378.1′662—dc22   2005004326

ISBN-13: 978-0618-57488-9

Book design by Hanley | Jones Art + Design

Manufactured in the United States of America
QUM   10 9 8 7 6 5 4 3 2 1

To all the students who have been
willing to skip and come back

Contents

Introduction

There is only one time when it is essential to awaken. That time is now.

—Buddha

What Is Zen and What Has It Got to Do with the SAT?

If you've heard the term *Zen* before, it might have been used in a sentence like "You just have to be Zen about it," which was offered as advice for getting through some unpleasant experience such as sitting at the kids' table at Thanksgiving. The implication is that Zen refers to an ability to endure through anything without much feeling—a way to zone out or just be mellow about everything. Nothing could be further from the truth.

Zen evolved over the last thousand years in Asia as a way to purify one's life through meditation. More recently, people around the world have taken a strong interest in Zen. Many

Americans, in particular, have found that the insights and practices of Japanese monks are effective antidotes to our stressed-out way of life.

Zen practice focuses on opening your mind to the present. Take a moment right now to hear all the sounds around you—traffic noise, birds, the hum of a refrigerator. Listening is a way to bring your attention into the present. Your mind rarely notices what you're hearing. Most of us dwell instead on thoughts that have nothing to do with the present. *What will she think about what I'm wearing? How will I ever get all my work done tonight? Why did my history teacher give me that grade? How can I get my parents to let me use the car?*

Zen teaches us that the thoughts that preoccupy us are not reality. As they clank around in our heads, reality goes on all around us. The goal of Zen practice is not so much to eliminate these thoughts as to become aware of their existence in our lives and to begin gently nudging them aside in order to give the present moment a larger place in our experience. When we let thoughts and worries about the past and future fall away, we become more aware of our existence in the moment, and we can concentrate on what's right in front of us. We also become aware of ourselves as part of a unity that is the universe.

Reading this book will not teach you to become one with the universe (though you may feel inspired to move in that direction on your own). The focus here is on a less global aspect of Zen practice known as *samadhi*, which means "being one with an object." In this case, the "object" we're talking about is a test: the SAT.

Samadhi is the state of mind that allows athletes and musicians to perform extraordinary feats. It allows lawyers to draft elegant contracts and artists to paint or draw or sculpt. *Samadhi* refers to a person's ability to bring total focus to a task through concentration. It is exactly the quality that the SAT demands.

A Critical Opportunity

How do you feel when you're taking a test and get a question about something you don't know? Your heart rate goes up. You might feel heat in your chest or your temples. If only you had read that chapter more carefully or memorized that formula— but now it seems there's little you can do. You make up some feeble nonsense in hopes of getting partial credit. Whether this happens to you all the time or almost never, it's one of the worst feelings you can experience as a student.

It's also something that you can count on experiencing while taking the SAT. However, on the SAT, this isn't necessarily a bad thing. It may even be a good thing.

In Japanese, the word for *crisis* (*kiki*) also means "critical opportunity." That's because every crisis can be a turning point. How you handle a crisis can make the difference between disaster and triumph.

At some point on the SAT, you may face a crisis—the anxiety caused by a question you initially *think* you can't answer. How you handle this crisis will determine how well you do. (And how you manage anxiety more generally will determine how well you do in lots of different things throughout life.) This book discusses the critical skills you need to do well on the SAT: reading, thinking, and managing anxiety. Reading and thinking are closely related on the test because many SAT questions can't be easily understood. Your brain has to break them down the way your stomach breaks down a pizza with too many toppings. From quirky math questions to complicated reading passages and the twenty-five-minute timed writing exercise, the challenges on the SAT can initially seem tricky if not impossible. Yet the guidance and suggestions offered here will teach you how to handle the test.

With the SAT, it's not enough to know the material. To excel on the SAT you must be confident about your ability to read carefully and solve problems—even strange, inscrutable ones—under timed conditions. That's what makes the SAT so intimidating. You can't just memorize the material and then regurgitate it; you have to act in the moment. Sure, there are some things you must know for the SAT. In fact, the new SAT is designed to include more content, like a school test. But the SAT will always demand less *knowing* than the tests you take at school and a lot more *figuring out*.

That's where Zen comes in. Zen practice trains us to bring our entire attention to the present moment while releasing the mind's hold on fragments from the past and future—ideas, worries, fears, and phantoms that can generate an endless stream of anxiety and self-doubt. You can learn how to manage anxiety in order to cultivate and sustain the presence of mind that will yield right answers because you are able in the heat of the moment to *figure out* even the toughest SAT problems.

As you move through *Zen in the Art of the SAT*, you'll first read about the nature of the test and discover how different the SAT is from the tests you are used to taking in school. Once you're clear about the nature of the test, you're ready to explore some of the primary obstacles many students face—issues connected with reading and anxiety—and how to overcome them. There are self-assessments that can help you gauge whether your reading habits are up to this challenge and what role anxiety plays in your test taking. There is also information that can help you make a study plan, and there's a section about parents. (You might want to encourage your parents to read it, too.) And, while the SAT is different from school tests and doesn't require that you memorize lots of material, there are some things you do need to know such as basic math, some rules of grammar and usage, and ways to approach timed essays. The section called "Some Things You Must Know" covers these basics.

For hundreds of years Zen practitioners have applied mental self-awareness techniques to everything from flower arranging to poetry. This book can help you apply similar ideas to the SAT. Since the test measures your ability to read, focus, and figure things out, sharpening your mental abilities can make a huge difference in your score and in how you *feel* about the test. Of course, the benefits of this work go beyond the test. The "Life Lessons" section shows how the best test preparation teaches valuable life lessons. As you learn how to ace the SAT, you will gain a deeper understanding of yourself and build your self-esteem and confidence. Additionally, you will discover how you can manage anxiety and turn what initially seems like a crisis into an opportunity. You will learn to do your best on the SAT not through any tricks or secret formulas but rather by getting a firm handle on the workings of your own mind.

Zen in the art of the SAT

I

The Nature of the Test

The koan* refuses to be solved under any [easy] conditions. But once solved the koan is compared to a piece of brick used to knock at a gate; when the gate is opened the brick is thrown away. The koan is useful as long as the mental doors are closed, but when they are opened it may be forgotten. What one sees after the opening will be something quite unexpected, something that has never before entered even into one's imagination. But when the koan is re-examined from this newly acquired point of view, how marvelously suggestive, how fittingly constructed, although there is nothing artificial here!

—D. T. Suzuki, *Zen Buddhism*

---

* Similar to a riddle but seemingly impossible to solve, koans are designed to reveal the true nature of reality.

1

In a Foreign Land

You have just finished the first semester of your sophomore year in college, and you're on a plane heading to Paris for what you anticipate will be the best two-week vacation of your life. This is the first trip you've taken by yourself, and you're thrilled to be on your own. Images of sitting in Parisian cafés and walking around famous museums fill your thoughts. You have never been to a foreign country before, but you are certain that you will feel at home. After all, you have been studying French for six years, and you're thinking about majoring in it.

Imagine your surprise when you discover that nobody appreciates your efforts to speak French. It starts right when you arrive at the airport and try to find a bus to take you to the youth hostel. The bus driver's rudeness begins to seem less awful when you compare it to the clerk's at the hostel. Finally you're checked in, but everything seems *really* different from home.

You aren't sure how the shower works, and you can't even figure out the phone to call your parents.

Refusing to abandon your romantic images of your trip to Paris, you head out to see the sights and eat exquisite French food. Quickly you are lost, unable to find the restaurant you circled in the guidebook. Everywhere you go, you think the locals are laughing at you, and you become too intimidated to try out your French. You even miss your parents at this point.

Taking the SAT is a lot like going to a foreign country by yourself. You will feel alone and lost—until you take the time to get to know the local scene. No matter how well prepared you are, knowing things in advance is not enough on the SAT. You must expect to do some poking around before you get comfortable with the questions.

Though you have undoubtedly taken many tests, the SAT is different from all of them. School tests measure what you know. When your teacher asks you to explain the causes of the Civil War, if you've studied and understood that chapter, you're in good shape. You write down what you know, and if you know the subject well and can write about it effectively, you will probably get full credit. But what if you haven't studied that chapter? What if you forgot the material? If you don't know the material, you're out of luck. It's not as if you're going to sit there and somehow figure it out during the test.

If you know basic math, can read at your grade level, and have solid writing skills, you have the knowledge you need for the SAT. But how do you "figure it out" when a question makes no sense? To do your best on the SAT, you must manage your anxieties and refocus your thoughts on the question. You must *get to know how your mind likes to work* on a problem and *train yourself to read with focus and attention.*

SAT questions aren't difficult—they're tricky and strange. They pose simple challenges in unfamiliar terms, or they combine familiar terms in unusual ways. There may be questions that *initially* seem to be written in a foreign language. All the knowledge in the world won't help you if you can't understand what the question is asking. The strangeness of the questions is what makes them difficult, not the material itself. Each question is like a little puzzle for you to figure out. And doing a puzzle takes patience and persistence as well as different strategies.

By the end of your two-week trip to Paris, you may still feel shaky and stressed, but you'll know your way around. You may even have a daily routine set up and know some of the locals in the neighborhood shops. You've figured out what you need to do to get your morning coffee and croissant and how to get to the Latin Quarter and the Eiffel Tower. Just as spending two weeks in Paris will allow you to improve your French and get introduced to the culture and customs of the country, becoming familiar and comfortable with the puzzles on the SAT will allow you to solve them—especially if you focus on building your reading and thinking skills as well as on managing your anxiety.

2

Walk Through the Open Door

In the movie *Cast Away*, Tom Hanks plays Chuck Noland, a FedEx executive who finds himself stranded on an uninhabited island when his plane crashes in the ocean. At first, Noland is devastated. He looks around hopelessly at his surroundings. What will he eat? How will he survive? Whether you've seen the movie or not, you know the story—it's the old one about the guy stuck on a desert island.

Hungry and thirsty, Noland notices the coconuts that litter the beach, but he can't get them open. He tries bashing them on rocks, but coconut shells are very, very hard. He gets frustrated, but his hunger and thirst overwhelm his frustration. He must open a coconut. He tries various strategies. Each failure seems to steel his determination, and quickly, instead of getting frustrated at a failure, he moves on to a new idea.

Opening a coconut soon becomes as routine to him as walking

on the beach. The trouble is that there are only so many coconuts you can eat. After a few days, he realizes that he'd better find some other things to eat, so he starts trying to catch fish. He goes through the same kind of process with catching the fish as he did with opening the coconuts. He tries everything he can think of until he finally finds a method that works.

Noland has no choice. If he wants to live, he has to eat. But the method he uses to overcome a series of overwhelmingly difficult situations is the same one you should use to solve the tougher questions on the SAT. Noland learns that continuing with an approach that hasn't worked is a waste of time and energy. Instead, he comes up with new strategies, using whatever tools his surroundings offer, and eventually he discovers what works.

The point is that in a room full of locked doors, you have to find the open door and walk through it. You may think there's something great behind one of those locked doors, but if you can't get to it, it's useless. The open door is the only one that provides a point of entry.

Watch how this works with the following SAT-type math question:

For how many three-digit integers will reversing the order of the digits yield a two-digit multiple of thirteen?

This is the type of question that stops many students cold. Panic sets in because they think that they don't know what the question means. Some students will start to put themselves down, saying to themselves, "I'm an idiot. I can't do this. I'm so stupid.

This test sucks." Move beyond judging yourself and the test and *focus* on the question.

If you take them one at a time, you probably know what all the words in this question mean. When they are presented all together in this arrangement, getting the meaning out of them on a first reading is about as difficult as getting the milk out of a coconut with your bare hands. You know it's there—tantalizingly close—but how do you get inside?

Now read the question again. This time, instead of worrying about what the whole thing means, look for open doors—pieces of the puzzle that make sense:

"For how many **three-digit integers**..." You know what a three-digit integer is—it's a number with three digits, like 747. Now take a moment to let that thought become even clearer.

You don't need to do anything clever. In fact, anything clever will probably mess this up. All you have to do is let your mind focus on what it already knows: three-digit numbers—what are they? They're all the numbers from 100 to 999.

Now what? "For how many three-digit integers will **reversing the order of the digits**..." Now that you have numbers you can try this: 325 becomes 523; 802 becomes 208.

Okay—that's not very useful. There are a ton of numbers (899, to be exact)—way too many to try them all out.

But you're not through. Keep reading (and keep looking for open doors): "For how many three-digit integers will reversing the order of the digits yield a **two-digit multiple of thirteen**." Here is another open door. You know how to get multiples of thirteen.

You may not know exactly why you're doing it, but walk through the open door. You know what "multiples of thirteen" means, so list the multiples of thirteen:

13, 26, 39, 52, 65, 78, 91...

104 is a multiple of thirteen, but it has three digits, and the question asks for two-digit multiples. So that's all of them.

Now that you have all the information laid out in front of you—having done only what came easily—you should be able to put all the pieces together and answer the question.

You need three-digit numbers that you can reverse to get the numbers 13, 26, 39, 52, 65, 78, and 91. How can you reverse a three-digit number and get a two-digit number? Easy—just add a zero: 310 becomes 013, also known as 13; 620 becomes 026—or 26.

Congratulations! You've cracked open the coconut. Now you're ready to go fishing!

The New SAT at a Glance

Math

CONTENT   Numbers and Operations

Algebra

Geometry

Data, Statistics, and Probability

TIME   70 minutes

(two 25-minute sections; one 20-minute section)

SCORE   200 – 800 points

Writing

CONTENT   Multiple-Choice Questions

(sentence errors, improving sentences and paragraphs)

Timed Essay

TIME   85 minutes

(two 25-minute sections; one 10-minute section;

one 25-minute essay)

SCORE   200 – 800 points

Critical Reading

CONTENT   Sentence Completions

Reading Passages

TIME   70 minutes

(two 25-minute sections; one 20-minute section)

SCORE   200 – 800 points

2400 Total Possible Points

The test always opens with the essay, followed by the twenty-five-minute sections and then the shorter sections. There are ten multiple-choice sections, including one experimental section, which does not count but is used by the test makers to try out new questions. The total time for the test, including the experimental section, is three hours and forty-five minutes.

You get a point for every right answer. You *lose* a quarter point for every wrong answer, but there is no penalty for leaving a question blank. (For an explanation of how the essay is scored, see Chapter 24.) Your point total for each section then gets translated into a scaled score between two hundred and eight hundred.

The biggest difference with the new SAT is the addition of the Writing section. This section used to be a separate test called the SAT II Writing. Students applying to top colleges took this test. Now everyone who takes the SAT I will do the Writing section.

The changes to the other sections are less dramatic. Analogies (cat : fur as fish : scales) and Quantitative Comparisons (column A/column B) are gone. The Math section adds some basic Algebra II content (negative exponents and simple functions). The Reading section now has short passages, which are one or two paragraphs in length.

II

Thinking

---

*Everything we do is an act of poetry or a painting
if we do it with mindfulness.*

—Thich Nhat Hanh

3

The Key to Better Thinking: Skip and Come Back

Ever think about thinking? When you have to think about something, how do you do it? What works? What doesn't work? It's easy to associate thinking with famous writers, philosophers, and scientists. Einstein liked to think. So did Virginia Woolf. But we're all thinkers.

Thinking is part of human nature. We all enjoy a good think—not the repetitive or chattering or obsessive mutterings of the mind, but deep-down, focused thinking. While growing up, I (Matt) used to lie in bed at night, thinking up elaborate stories about animals and their underground habitats. There were good animals and bad ones. Every night, I would come up with a new way for the good animals to *almost* lose their battles. It took a lot of ingenuity to bring these squirrels, monkeys, and birds to the brink of disaster without pushing them over, because the closer they came to losing, the better the story. Nowadays, I try to stop myself from thinking about fantasy baseball.

Some people like to think about their friends. People watch game shows and try to outthink the contestants. You may think about politics or art or history or business or movies or technology or religion or math or fashion.

Whatever you like to think about, preparing for the SAT offers an opportunity to improve *how* you think. The test makes clear that when you're trying to solve a problem, the best way to think is in stages. Of course, this is true well beyond the test. Our brains work better when we give them more than one shot at a problem.

If you have ever taken music lessons, you know what it's like to get up in front of a group of mostly strangers and perform at a recital. The big day finally arrives. You've practiced for what seems like a lifetime. You know exactly which parts of the piece are going to be difficult, so you've given extra attention to those.

Your dad is in the audience. He's so excited that he made your grandparents drive three hours to share the moment. The audience finishes applauding for the kid who plays before you. She's done. It's your turn.

You walk out to the piano, pull the bench out—it squeaks as if you've broken it or something—and sit down. Someone coughs in the audience. You don't dare take your eyes off those keys. *This is your one shot. Now or never. Do or die.* When you were rehearsing, you often made little mistakes. You ignored them and kept playing. But here, one slip of your fingers and everything you've worked for will be wasted. The audience will gasp. You will keep it together and finish, but later you will feel awful.

Everyone will tell you it's okay, but you will feel it isn't. For a brief instant before your fingers touch the keys, an image of yourself lying on your bed at home with a big bag of Cheetos and a soda fills your mind. All you want to do is get through your piece and get out of there. And that's exactly what you do. You don't put much feeling into it, but you get through it.

For many students, the SAT feels like a piano recital. Everything is on the line (maybe even more so than at a piano recital). It may seem as if any little mistake could undermine everything you've worked so hard to achieve throughout high school. In truth, a lot is at stake when you take this test. But there is one HUGE difference.

Nobody is watching *how* you do your test. When you come to a question you don't like, *you don't have to answer it right away.* Imagine a figure skating competition in which the skaters got to stop in the middle of their jumps if they didn't go well, move on to different parts of their routines, and then come back later and nail the jumps.

That's what you can do on the SAT. Sure, the pressure is on, but when you find a question that's difficult for you, you can pause, fast-forward, and rewind. You don't have to do this question right away. Your time may be limited, but you get to control how you use it.

The best way to use your time is to *skip* and *come back* to any questions that give you trouble. This may seem counterintuitive at first. If you don't know a question right away, how will it help to come back to it later? Your experience on school tests has trained you to believe that your success depends on knowing the answer right away. If you don't remember what the endoplasmic reticulum does, you can't get the question right.

But the SAT is different. You don't have to *know everything right away*. You have to *figure stuff out*. You get right answers on the SAT by reading the questions and *thinking through* what they mean.

When you come to a tough question, you may feel a wall of frustration and anxiety coming down. How you handle that wall will determine how you do on the test. Even if you want to give up, your next instinct may be to *keep trying*. Don't do it. Respect the wall, which is *not* the same thing as giving in to it. When you're frustrated, the harder you try, the *less* likely you are to discover the right answer. If you linger too long on a difficult question, you make the wall bigger. You need a fresh take on the material, but you will never get it by staying put.

You increase your chance of succeeding by quickly getting away from a tough question, distracting yourself with a few more questions, and then coming right back with an open mind. Visiting and revisiting the trickiest questions puts your mind at ease. The wall shrinks and so you can read the questions more clearly and get comfortable with them. Each time you reread a question, you give your brain a fresh shot at it. Given the chance, your brain will do what it was made to do: think. As you work your way through a section of the test, you will find that you develop a natural thinking rhythm that actually feels good.

Don't be afraid to come back to problems more than once. It's best to arrive at the more difficult problems at the end of a section with several questions to go back to. That way you have something to distract yourself with when you have to skip the ones at the end.

Keep in mind the Chinese fable about the river with the boulder blocking its path. The boulder is too big for the river to lift out of the way, so the river flows around it. But the river does not give up on getting rid of the boulder. On the contrary, the waters flowing past the stone gradually wear it away until it's gone. Imagine yourself as that steady, consistent river, returning again and again to wear away any obstacles to answering the question.

Skip-and-Come-Back Fact Sheet

The first time you try something new is the hardest.

If you get frustrated but keep trying anyway, you will almost never succeed.

If you get frustrated but keep trying anyway, you waste time.

If you get frustrated but keep trying anyway, you lose momentum.

If you get frustrated but keep trying anyway, you get a hang-up about the problem.

If you get frustrated but keep trying anyway, you undermine your confidence.

Losing momentum and confidence makes it harder to get the next question.

The second time you try something it gets easier.

The second time you try something you have a better handle on it.

The second time you read something it comes into clearer focus.

Each time you come back and try something, you get better at it.

4

When to Skip and When to Come Back

When I (Matt) was in high school, I had a construction job on a local college campus, assisting a Guatemalan contractor named Hermelio. At barely five feet tall, with big, brown, watery eyes from too much smoking, Hermelio was famous for being the hardest-working guy around. Though he was sixty-four years old at the time, Hermelio still routinely tossed fifty-pound bags of cement.

He was also famous for being disgusted with how lazy he thought everyone else was. He was an impossible guy to work for—or so I initially thought. He didn't speak English. He would bark out instructions in staccato bursts of Spanish, which he expected his workers to understand and obey. And he expected everyone to work as hard as he did—all day long.

I'll never forget my first day with Hermelio. The manager brought me in and introduced me. Hermelio barely looked up.

He was replacing bathroom tiles. He was on his knees, covered in dust, a lit cigarette dangling from his lips. The manager shrugged and left me to my fate.

For the first hour and a half, Hermelio said nothing. He didn't even look at me. I just stood there. I wanted to sit down, but I didn't want him to think I was a slacker. Finally, without looking at me, he croaked out something that sounded like "Marty O'Since." "*Que?*" I responded. "What?"

"Marty O'Since!" He was starting to get annoyed, but I had no idea what he wanted. He kept shouting at me—"Marty O'Since! Marty O'Since!"—and gesturing at a pile of tools on the other side of the room. I began picking up tools and offering them, which made him even angrier. Finally, he took the hammer from me (*martillo* in Spanish) and, shaking his head in disgust, went and grabbed the chisel (*cinsel*) himself. Not a promising start.

After a few days, I started to understand some of what he was saying to me. Despite a rocky beginning, I gradually won his respect with my hard work. And once you won Hermelio's respect, you had a permanent place in his heart.

Much of my job consisted of hauling stuff back and forth in a wheelbarrow from Hermelio's shed to whatever job he was doing. I prided myself on making as few trips as possible, preferring to stack the wheelbarrow high with hundreds of pounds of supplies and tools.

One day, Hermelio looked up at me struggling under a heavy load and said, "Teo (short for Mateo), *no trabaje fuerte.*"

("Matt, don't work hard.") *"Malo...muy malo."* ("It's bad...
very bad.")

I thought he was joking, but his expression was serious, as if
he was telling me something important. What was he talking
about? Hermelio Gomez was the definition of hard work. This
man, who worked from dawn till dusk with hardly a break, was
telling me that it was bad to work hard. I stared at him, dumb-
founded.

He stubbed out his Marlboro and looked at me. "Work," he
said. "Never hard. Just keep working." Then I got it. Steady,
consistent work, not backbreaking work, was what he did.

When to Skip

There's no heavy lifting on the SAT. Solving even the most
challenging SAT questions involves nothing more than accurately reading and understanding what's on the page.

When you sense the load increasing on your brain, *skip*.
Skip right away. Skip before you feel ready to skip. Skip at the
slightest whiff of trouble. If you've read a question twice and
still don't know what it means, skip. If you've answered the
question but suddenly realize you may have misread something, skip! Just as I learned to make several trips with the
wheelbarrow when moving supplies and tools, you too must
learn to avoid trying to move everything at once. Skip and come
back and work steadily.

The thinking part of your brain is like a child at play. If you
try to force her to do something, no matter how reasonable the

request, she won't do it. When she starts to get frustrated with an activity, if you want to hold her interest, you would do well to move her on to another activity where she can succeed *before* she has a fit.

When to Come Back

Skipping and coming back works because you distract yourself from a tough question by focusing on other questions. Then, when you come back to the tough one, you bring a fresh perspective and avoid reading it again in exactly the same way that didn't work before. Come back soon to the questions you have skipped, after doing three or four more problems, not at the end of the whole section. If you wait until the end of the section to come back, you will find that you have completely forgotten the question. You will be pressed for time, and your anxieties will cancel the benefits of seeing the problem again.

5

Beginner's Mind: How to Come Back

Being a beginner reminds me (Susan) of Red Cross swimming lessons, where everyone desperately wanted to leave the beginners' group (aka the Tadpoles) as soon as possible. Anything was better than being stuck in the shallow end or, worse, having to wear water wings.

Why would anyone ever want to be a beginner? Many things about Zen are puzzling. What might be most surprising is the appeal of what is called "beginner's mind."

In Zen practice everyone always strives to be a beginner. Nobody gets rid of water wings and swims off to the deep end, and nobody wants to. The beginner's mind is open and fresh and full of possibilities.

The beginner's mind is the original mind, the mind that is rich and self-sufficient. This mind is empty and ready for anything. It is open to everything. This is the mind that you need each time you return to a question on the SAT.

Imagine you discover a song that speaks to you. As you listen to the song over and over, will you lose the wonderful way you felt when you first heard this song? Beginner's mind is what allows you to retain the original excitement you had when you first discovered that song. It's also what prevents you from becoming an expert, someone who knows everything and so stops finding new things in what is familiar.

Imagine that you are going to approach the SAT with beginner's mind. Envision yourself coming back to problems that seemed impossible and approaching them with an open mind. You return to the problems over and over until what you need to solve them suddenly becomes clear to you. Imagine that you do this without drama or delay.

6

Reasons Not to Skip and Come Back (and Why They're Wrong)

At first, skipping a question you think you can get will seem wrong. It may feel like quitting. Why skip if you think you might be able to get the answer? But you're not quitting. You're going to come right back. You're simply giving your brain a fresh shot at the question.

You may feel that skipping won't help because when you come back, you'll have to face the same confusion again. Okay, maybe that will be true at first. But if you can keep an open mind, *if you can practice beginner's mind,* you will find that even a couple of minutes away will give your brain a fresh perspective it cannot acquire if you stay locked on to the question.

You may feel this strategy will take too much time. It won't. Compared to the precious minutes wasted staring at a question you don't understand, the few seconds you take to reread a problem are nothing. The real waste of time on the SAT is the downtime spent puzzling and wondering about a question you simply don't understand *at first*. If you move efficiently through each section of the test, answering only what you can read and understand clearly and coming back repeatedly to the ones that give you trouble, you'll have plenty of time.

7

An Example: Erica Works the Test

Erica goes to a big suburban high school. She and her friends in the honors track usually downplay their successes in school. They tend to be more competitive about things like *Simpsons* or *South Park* expertise than they are about grades. But for some reason, they've got a bet going about who will get the highest SAT score. Erica's strength is on the Math sections.

When I (Matt) tutored Erica, she was skeptical at first about skipping and coming back. It didn't feel right to her. She loved to prove me wrong by refusing to move on from a difficult question and then getting it right anyway. "See," she would say, with a glint in her eye, "I didn't need to skip." When I pointed out that she could have gotten the answer more efficiently by skipping and coming back, Erica just shrugged and smiled.

A pattern formed. On practice tests, Erica stubbornly refused to skip and come back to math questions (though the strategy worked well for her on Reading sections), but she kept missing two or three questions at the end of each Math section. As her test date approached, Erica got more and more frustrated. She told me she was about ready to give up. I just laughed and shook my head. "Erica," I said, "why don't you try it my way?" In a fit of desperation, she finally did. Here's how it happened.

She was working on a practice section when she came to this question:

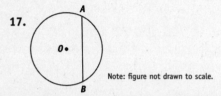

17.

Note: figure not drawn to scale.

In the figure above, radius *OC* bisects chord *AB* at point *D* (not shown). If the length of chord *AB* is 12, and the circle has radius 10, what is the distance along the radius from point *D* to the circumference?

Obviously, this is a difficult problem. When Erica read it, she rolled her eyes and made a face. I invited her to notice what she was feeling—dejection, hopelessness—and then to set her feelings aside and get to work.

Erica read number 17 again, and suddenly she had an idea. "Oh, this is easy," she said. She drew in the radius bisecting chord *AB*:

She read the problem again and labeled point *D* at the intersection of the chord and the new radius she had drawn.

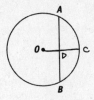

"It looks like about six, but I have no idea how to do this. I think there's a formula..." she said. I shook my head.

"Skip."

"But I know I can get this one," she pleaded.

"I know you can get it, too," I replied. "The question is *how*. Now move on. There are other questions waiting for you, and the clock's ticking." After some minor whining and eye rolling, she did what I suggested.

I knew that for a kid like Erica who was used to getting math questions right, moving on felt like failure. I felt bad for her, but my job was to help her succeed, and I also knew that if I let her stay with the problem, she would probably get more and more frustrated and never get it right.

There were only three more questions in the section. Erica got one of them, the second-to-last question, but struggled on the other two. For some reason, however—maybe she felt too defeated to resist—she didn't argue anymore but agreed instead to move on right away from the two she wasn't getting. It was then time to face number 17 again.

17.

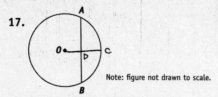

Note: figure not drawn to scale.

In the figure above, radius *OC* bisects chord *AB* at point *D* (not shown). If the length of chord *AB* is 12, and the circle has radius 10, what is the distance along the radius from point *D* to the circumference?

She had spent only a couple of minutes away from the problem, but even that small window gave Erica a fresh start. She began to notice details she had overlooked the first time through.

"I have no idea how this helps, but the two halves of the chord are each six," she said. She labeled them.

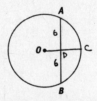

"And I think those angles at *D* are right angles."

On the more difficult problems, there are usually intermediate steps on the way to the right answer. I knew that if she didn't waste time getting frustrated, any work Erica did on the problem would move her closer to the right answer.

"What else do you know?" I asked.

"Nothing. The radius is ten. That's it," she said.

"Good work!" I reassured her. "You took a step closer and gained a better understanding. And it didn't take you long, either."

"Yeah, great, but I didn't get the answer."

"You're missing the point. Every good step doesn't result in an answer—at least not right away."

"So how do I solve it?"

I smiled and gestured for her to move on.

Erica rolled her eyes again but did as I said. I could sense a tiny but essential change. She was starting to work the test. She skipped number 18 again, then quickly got number 20.

"That was dumb," she commented. "How did I miss that one before?"

"You weren't dumb," I corrected her. "It's just easier to see the problem and the answer the second time through."

Back to 17.

17.

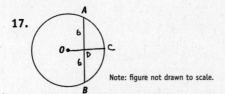

Note: figure not drawn to scale.

In the figure above, radius *OC* bisects chord *AB* at point *D* (not shown). If the length of chord *AB* is 12, and the circle has radius 10, what is the distance along the radius from point *D* to the circumference?

Erica got a new idea: "Right angles...I can use the Pythagorean theorem!" She drew in a hypotenuse:

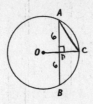

"So one side is six…" Then her face fell. "It's not enough. I need another side."

Before any more air could leak out of her enthusiasm balloon, I made her skip again. I reminded her that there was still one other problem for her to get and that she won't get any extra points for spending all her time on this one, even if it was extremely tricky and challenging.

She went back to 18 and, with a little more poking and prodding, found the answer to it.

Now all she had left was number 17. I reminded her to let go of her frustrations and keep her mind open to everything on the page, both the question itself and all the good work she had done.

17.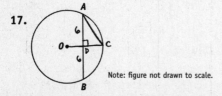

Note: figure not drawn to scale.

In the figure above, radius _OC_ bisects chord _AB_ at point _D_ (not shown). If the length of chord _AB_ is 12, and the circle has radius 10, what is the distance along the radius from point _D_ to the circumference?

As she reread the question, she noticed again that the figure was not drawn to scale. "I wonder what's off about it?" she asked. "It looks fine...Wait a minute. The radius is ten. The way it's drawn makes the chord look way longer than the radius, when actually, it's only a little bit longer." She redrew the circle:

She added the radius and labeled everything:

Then she saw it. Erica smiled. She drew another hypotenuse and labeled it:

She now had two sides. She used the Pythagorean theorem $(a^2 + b^2 = c^2)$ to solve for the length of the missing side:

$6^2 + x^2 = 10^2$

$36 + x^2 = 100$

$x^2 = 64$

$x = 8$

The third side of the right triangle was 8.

Since the length of the entire radius *OC* was 10, the length of *DC* was 2.

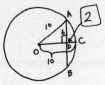

8

From "I Can't" to "I Can"

If the test makers gave you a list of specific facts you needed to learn and then tested you on only these facts, the SAT might be a lot easier. Instead, you can count on coming to a question somewhere in each section of the test for which you not only don't know the answer but also don't understand what the question means. Not having any idea what the question means feels scary, perhaps even terrifying. On an important test in school, if you don't know what the question means, it's usually your fault. You were supposed to study. There's a sickening feeling when that happens on a school test. It feels like failure.

The same is true on the SAT, but the feeling of failure gets magnified by the pressure of the moment and the annoying simplicity of the questions. You know that the right answers are *right there*. If only they would come to you.

For Erica, the sudden appearance of a failure, especially after so many reassuring successes, dropped a blanket of frustration and fear over her mind. "I can't," she told herself. "I can't do this."

There is a finality about this thought that would be ridiculous if it weren't so self-fulfilling. Given what we know about the simplicity of even the most challenging SAT questions, it's pretty silly for anyone to feel so sure she can't do one. But once those two little words got loose in Erica's mind—*I can't*—they bounced around, stirring up a storm of anxiety that felt irreversible. Once that switch got flipped, it became hard to flip it back.

The obvious solution is never to tell yourself, "I can't." Think positively. Keep your chin up. But if it were that easy, we'd all get perfect scores without even trying. "I can't" is part of life, and we all have this thought at one time or another.

The right approach to the SAT can teach you to minimize the damage from "I can't" and turn it around into "I can." Here's how:

1. *Don't expect to go straight to the answer.* When you're looking at a tricky question and your mind is saying, "I can't," telling yourself that you can will often not work. "I can't" happens because you've lost your rhythm. You've fallen out of your groove. You'll have to reestablish a level of comfort before the question can become clear again.

2. *Skip and come back.* The longer you hang out on a question with the words "I can't" dancing around in your head, the more you blunt your momentum and the harder it becomes

to see what you've missed. Getting yourself focused on a different question quickly gets you back in your rhythm and minimizes the damage to your confidence.

3. *"Let's see" and "Maybe I can."* These are the phrases you want rattling around your mind when you come back to a question that might otherwise make you say, "I can't." If you return to the question and you're still convinced that you can't figure it out, you won't. By doing several other questions, you've put your confidence back together and gotten back into your rhythm. Now you can bring a fresh approach to a challenging problem. Even if you still don't understand the problem, you can at least say, "Let's see."

4. *From "Maybe I can" to "I can."* Once you've gotten back into your rhythm, you give yourself the opportunity to see what you missed the last time around. Maybe you misread something. Maybe there's a strategy you can use that you didn't notice before. (See the chapters in the section called "Some Things You Must Know" for lots of strategies.) Whatever it is, you are now giving yourself the opportunity to find it.

5. *Results.* If you get the question right, make sure you notice how you did it. What did you miss the first time around? See if you can figure out why. How did you finally get it? If you never did figure it out, go over the right answer later and find out what went wrong. By seeing what you missed as you work on practice tests, you'll come to understand the nature of the

test and gain a better understanding of the challenges you'll face the next time around.

Each time you practice the progression from "I can't" to "Let's see" to "Maybe I can" to "I can" to results, you get a little better at thinking. The "I can't" moments begin to shrink in duration and intensity.

You may never stop thinking "I can't," but the more familiar you get with the workings of this mechanism in your brain, the less scary it will seem. You'll learn to anticipate and deal with it so that the moments of "I can't" will become less frequent and less significant.

Anarchy

Some people are like mad dogs who bark at every passing breeze.

—Huang Po

Do you have the patience to wait until the mud settles?

—Zen saying

9

The Buddha and the SAT

Anxiety:...2. Psychiatry *A state of apprehension, uncertainty, and fear*
resulting from the anticipation of a realistic or fantasized threatening
event or situation, often impairing physical and psychological functioning.

—*American Heritage Dictionary,* fourth edition

Siddhartha Gautama, the only son of a royal family in India, lived
about 2,500 years ago. When he was a newborn, his father, King
Suddhodhana, invited a group of priests to predict Siddhartha's
future. They told the king that his son would either become a
great and powerful ruler or a wise spiritual guide. The king
wanted his son to become the greatest ruler in the world and did
all that he could to prevent Siddhartha from taking the spiritual
path. He spoiled his son and kept him from ever entering the
world beyond the palace grounds. As Siddhartha grew up, he

became a good student, a talented athlete, and a well-liked and respected young man. It wasn't until he was about twenty-nine years old that he ever left the palace grounds and discovered the world beyond all his luxuries and riches.

As he ventured outside his familiar home, Siddhartha began to realize that the world was full of suffering. Nothing in his rich and abundant life could comfort him as he began to worry about the pain in life, particularly that which comes with death. Though he had many of the things most people long for—fame, power, money, love, good health, education—he couldn't accept this life, knowing that there was so much suffering in the world. He headed out on a journey to search for a deeper truth.

One day he found himself remembering an afternoon he had spent under an apple tree as a young and carefree boy. He realized that the bliss he felt then had come from the sheer joy of being fully in that moment. The memory led him to become ever more conscious of himself, and he began to note his every movement and its effect on the world. In becoming mindful of his actions and gestures, he realized how quickly everything changed. Change, he realized, was inevitable. In continuing to observe himself and the world, Siddhartha kept noticing the connections that link all the world's different parts. Sitting under a bodhi tree, he contemplated how the fruit on the tree was nourished by the earth, where the roots of the tree were planted.

He continued to observe the interrelationships within the natural world and their inevitable changes, and he concluded that nothing was ever permanent. Yet he also noted that while everything would die, it would also be replaced by something else. As he sat under the bodhi tree, observing the world and meditating, he began to liberate himself from his own petty concerns. His thoughts and worries disappeared, and he found himself living fully in the present moment. Even though he was far from his father's riches and now barely had enough to eat, Siddhartha experienced a more profound satisfaction. He fully understood what had been available to him and every other human being all along: his own tiny place in the present moment and its connection to everything else in the marvelous and infinite universe.

On reaching enlightened mind, Siddhartha became the Buddha, or the "Enlightened One." Knowing that he couldn't sit under the bodhi tree forever, he soon set out to spread his teachings. He had to talk with other people and teach them how to find enlightenment for themselves. It was from the Buddha's teachings that Zen evolved, and for dozens of generations since, practitioners of Zen have sought to improve life by fully experiencing the present moment.

The principles of Zen can help you handle one of the SAT's biggest hurdles: anxiety. When anxiety hits, it removes us from the present moment and fills our heads with bad experiences from the past and fears about the future. Zen practice teaches us to guide our minds gently but constantly back to the present. Zen habits steer us clear of anxiety's traps and toward a fuller expression of our real abilities.

Take a moment now to notice the present moment. What do you hear? Birds? Traffic? Other people? What do you see? Colors? Patterns? Notice the quality of light and shadow. Feel the texture of the book in your hands and notice the contact your body is making with whatever you're sitting or lying on. Sniff the air. Can you distinguish any smells? What taste do you have in your mouth?

All of these elements make up your experience of the present moment. You have the same access to the present moment that Siddhartha had under the bodhi tree 2,500 years ago. Anything else going on in your head—the math homework you haven't done, what you're having for dinner, worries, fantasies—most of it is not the present moment.

Focusing on the present moment takes the teeth out of anxiety.

10

Anxiety and the Present Moment

When you're in a state of anxiety, nothing works. You can't think. You can't read. And even if you can, you don't understand or remember what you're reading. Studies have shown that anxiety causes blood vessels in the brain to shrink and consequently limit the flow of oxygen. Sometimes when one feels intense anxiety, even something as basic as breathing becomes difficult.

There are many causes for anxiety about the SAT. Parents, peer pressure, and sibling rivalries all play parts. Societal pressures about college and fantasies about the status you'll gain or lose from the college admissions process also contribute. But perhaps the biggest source of anxiety is the test itself. As Alice, a junior in high school from Brooklyn, New York, put it, "It just seems unfair that people are going to judge you based on how you do on one single test."

The nature of the test makes it stressful. You can't prepare for the SAT in the usual way. You're used to tests on which you do well if you study hard enough. This test seems far more out of your control because studying the material doesn't always guarantee good results.

For almost all of us, the SAT forces us to confront the fragile nature of our self-confidence. Somewhere during the test, every student, no matter how well prepared, confronts a question she or he does not understand. Nobody likes to fail, and because we expect our studying to prepare us for every question on a test, reading a question without understanding how to do it *feels* like failure.

Of course, none of this is real. Consider the definition of anxiety: "... apprehension, uncertainty, and fear resulting from the anticipation of a ... threatening event or situation." What "event or situation"? Is it accurate to believe that a low score on the SAT will lead to failure in life? Will your life spiral downward from this moment?

Probably not. The world is full of successful people who bombed the SAT. There's a lot to be said for doing well on the test, but what we imagine will happen if we fail is just that— imaginary. Imaginings of doom and gloom, however, can make it even harder to do well on the test. In any case, all of these concerns go away when you engage the present moment. The only thing that counts when you're taking the SAT is the question on the page right in front of you.

Zen teaches us to tune out distractions in order to experience the present moment. All the stuff you think about when you're panicking on a test is, in fact, not a real part of taking the test. The sounds of traffic outside, the low hum of a ventilation system, the words on the page—these are all real. No matter how substantive or how real your fears may feel, they are not real. The only reality that matters on the test is *your mind's grasp of the words on the page*. If you constantly take your attention away from unreal distractions and return it to the words on the page, to the simple experience of reading and comprehending the meaning that the words represent, your anxieties will melt away. You can train your mind to fight through all distractions, including anxiety. This is where *samadhi* comes in. Through moving your attention back to the test whenever it strays and being mindful of only what's directly in front of you, you can bring total focus to this task.

Of course, we don't expect you to become a Zen master between now and the SAT, but practicing a more meditative approach to test taking, in which you get used to gently moving your attention away from distractions and back to the text, will help reduce anxieties. So will raising your reading level, taking practice tests, reviewing basic math concepts, reviewing grammar and usage rules, and talking with parents or friends who may be feeding your anxieties. The best way to deal with anxieties, however, is to plan on having them and to be honest about them.

Anxiety is a part of life. Trying to get rid of anxiety is like trying to get rid of germs. While there are many productive steps you can take, the only way to avoid exposure to germs completely is to seal yourself in a sterilized plastic bubble. That's not to say, however, that there's nothing you can do to *manage* anxieties or that you have to take drastic measures such as the plastic bubble. During the last hundred years, since doctors discovered that bacteria and viruses cause most illnesses, the biggest advance in disease prevention has been the washing of hands— a simple ritual that has a far more significant effect than vaccines or medical cures.

Just as washing hands simply but effectively helps your body fight germs, breathing and meditation techniques (along with skipping and coming back) help your mind fight anxiety.

11
Breathing

What we call "I" is just a swinging door which moves when we inhale and when we exhale.

—Shunryu Suzuki, *Zen Mind, Beginner's Mind*

It's the first and last thing we do on this earth. In between, we take approximately 750 million breaths. Some are shallow and some are deep. Some are quick and some are slow. Most happen easily and naturally. A few come with great effort.

Zen practitioners focus on the breath as a way to connect as closely as possible with the present moment. One of the first tasks of Zen meditation is to bring awareness to your breathing. In many cultures, breathing has been used as a way to access and affect one's internal state. Consciously altering the pattern of the breath can lead to a sense of calm and well-being.

Let's be realistic. Reducing anxiety through breathing techniques may be extremely effective, but it's also difficult to do. This chapter isn't about instant results. Still, since breathing is such a basic tool in any effort to reduce anxiety, it's probably worth finding out more about it.

One way your brain deals with stress or anger is to tighten various muscles throughout your body. They could be big muscles, like the ones in your lower back, or small ones, like those in your temples or at the base of your tongue. Your mind does this automatically, without asking for your permission first.

After a while, your muscles get tired. They don't get enough oxygen, and this causes them to release lactic acid, a substance that creates anything from mild discomfort to severe pain. In order to relax, your muscles need new instructions from your brain, and they need oxygen.

Take a moment right now to notice your body. Repeat the following exercise at different moments, such as when you're resting, before a test, and even when you're having an argument. Where do you feel tension? Notice your feet, calves, and knees. Notice your thighs, hips, and lower back. Bring your attention to your upper back, shoulders, arms, and hands. Notice any tension in your neck, throat, head, face, and mouth.

Take a nice, slow inhalation and, as you do, instruct the parts of your body that are tense to let go. Acknowledge the stress and/or anger that you are feeling and reassure yourself that you don't have to tense your feet or shoulders or lower back. Try to inhale through your nose and exhale slowly through your mouth. The inhale guides oxygen to overworked and tense muscles. The exhale carries tensions away with your outgoing breath. As you do these exercises, you influence your nervous system and center your mind.

After you've done this a few times, begin to notice where your breath is going. Do you breathe into the bottoms of your lungs? The middle? Or does your inhaling fill the upper part of your chest? Try breathing to the bottoms and then to the tops of your lungs.

Notice the space at the base of your throat where the collarbone dips down to meet the sternum. There's a little depression where your collarbone ends and your windpipe goes down into your chest. Pretend you can breathe in through that spot and slowly fill first the upper parts of your lungs and then the lower parts. Exhale slowly and release tension as you go.

You may not feel instantly soothed by doing this, but if you practice you will find what works for you. During the test, there may not be enough time to do this entire exercise, but it's a good one for the tense moments while you're waiting for the test to begin or while you're in between sections. Also, if you feel yourself begin to tense up because you have come to a particularly tough question, take a few deep breaths. You do have time to do that. Keep yourself calm by following Dr. Andrew Weil's advice that you make your breathing "deeper, slower, quieter, and more regular." Dr. Weil, a Western-trained medical doctor who directs an integrative medicine program at the University of Arizona, believes that "breathing is the master key to self healing." During the test, notice your breath. If it becomes rapid or shallow, slow it down. Your brain will do its best work if your breathing is "deep, slow, quiet, and regular."

Another breathing exercise you can try any time you need to boost your energy and focus is the "6-4-6-1: The Energizing Breath." You can even use it during the test. Take a long inhalation through your nose, counting slowly (in your head) up to six. Try to fill your lungs steadily as you go. Hold the breath as you count slowly to four, and then exhale completely through the mouth counting slowly to six. Pause for one beat, neither inhaling nor exhaling, and then repeat the exercise. Do this several times in succession and see how it affects your energy.

Use these exercises throughout your preparation—whenever you find yourself sinking into imaginary scenarios of doom and gloom. The more you bring breathing exercises into your everyday life, the more likely that you will remember to use them when tension hits.

12

Basic Meditation: Managing Anxiety

Meditation can be practiced almost anywhere—while sitting,
walking, lying down, standing, even while working, drinking,
and eating. Sitting is only the most familiar form of meditation.

—Thich Nhat Hanh, *The Blooming of the Lotus*

A little bit of meditation goes a long way. You may want to use only a few of the exercises in this chapter, or you may use all of them, but any of this will help you be more relaxed and focused on the SAT and in everyday life.

Often anxiety can lead us to have what Zen practitioners call "monkey mind." The idea is that your mind jumps from thought to thought just as a monkey jumps from branch to branch. When you have monkey mind, your mind is cluttered and your thoughts are jumbled. Meditation provides a means for quieting monkey mind. In the last chapter we focused on breathing, which is at the heart of meditation. Here we extend and develop those ideas in order to provide additional ways to quiet anxiety and return your focus to the present moment.

Step One

Sit quietly for about a minute. Don't *do* anything. Turn off your computer, MP3 player, cell phone, land line, TV. Make sure you're sitting, not lying down. Use a hard chair and sit up straight. Let your hands rest on your knees. Notice sounds. Keep your eyes open. Notice your surroundings. Notice thoughts. You may feel sad or angry or excited or tired. Just notice these feelings but continue to sit without doing anything. Try to stay awake, but if you start to fall asleep, that's okay. Do this every day for a few days, adding a little more time each day, but make sure you start out slowly. You will get more out of this exercise if you let yourself build up gradually. Work toward practicing this exercise for 10–15 minutes every day.

Step Two

Carry the habit of noticing the present moment into your daily routine. At various moments during the day, whenever you get the chance, notice everything you can about the present moment: sights, sounds, feelings, thoughts. Check in with all five senses. Notice colors and patterns. Notice the little inconsistencies that make each moment unique: the smudge on the wall, the sounds of machines or the rain outside or wind or the hum of lights, the insect crawling on the dashboard. Notice light and darkness.

Notice things that may be upsetting you and things that are making you happy. They could be big things like relationships with important people in your life or trivial matters like the way a piece of clothing looks. Again, don't *do* anything. Just notice.

Step Three

Find a quiet, calming place in your home. If no such place exists, do the best you can to create one, perhaps even one you can come back to frequently. Put a pillow on the floor and sit down on it. Bring your attention to the present moment, but this time focus on your breathing. Take a long, slow inhalation, counting slowly up to three. Hold the breath, taking another slow three counts. Then exhale slowly, again counting to three. Do this once and then breathe normally. Bring your attention to your breath. If you want, you may count breaths, but after the first one, don't manage or control them. Just let your lungs do their work. This may be very difficult at first.

As you notice yourself getting distracted, don't get upset. Gently return your focus to your breathing. Notice any thoughts you have by labeling them. "That's a thought," tell yourself, and return your attention to your breathing. At first, try this for two or three minutes once a day. Doing more may frustrate you. When you're ready to stop, repeat the controlled inhalation, hold, and exhalation. As you get more comfortable, extend your three counts to five and finally to eight. You may also want to extend the duration of the exercise. Some people meditate for long stretches of time, but five minutes once a day is enough to make a huge difference.

13

Assessing Your Anxiety

Use the following assessment to identify the factors that contribute to your own anxiety about the SAT. Take your time answering these questions and be honest.

1. What SAT score would make me happy? What score would I feel confident sending to colleges? (Be honest with yourself about this. Your answer should be a number between, say, 1200 and 2400—the sum of your three scores on the Critical Reading, Math, and Writing sections. For example, a 650 on the Critical Reading, a 550 on the Math, and a 600 on the Writing would give you 1800.)

2. What is my current PSAT score? (Again, the number you put down here should be the sum of all three subscores: Critical Reading, Writing, and Math. Multiply your answer by ten so that it looks like an SAT score.)

3. Subtract the answer to question 2 from the answer to question 1.

4. When I get a bad grade in school, I usually (put a check next to all that apply)

   a. feel awful.
   b. feel it was unfair.
   c. don't care.
   d. complain to the teacher.
   e. complain to my parent(s).
   f. do better on the next test or assignment.
   g. do the same or worse on the next test or assignment.
   h. review my mistakes carefully and thoughtfully.
   i. throw the offending test or assignment in the trash without looking at it.
   j. I have never gotten a bad grade.

5. Write the number of times per week that each of the following sentences might come to mind:

   a. "I'm such a loser."
   b. "I'm stupid."
   c. "I'm reliable" or "I'm capable."
   d. "I'm better than others around me."
   e. "Everything's okay with me."
   f. "I'm incompetent."
   g. "Everyone's smarter than I am."
   h. "I'll never get what I want."

6. On a scale from 1 to 10, these people in my life either consciously or unconsciously increase my anxiety about the SAT
(a 1 means they cause almost no anxiety and a 10 means they
make me crazy about the test almost every day):

   a. Friends
   b. Siblings
   c. Parent(s)

Note: If there is one individual who stands out in any one category, the score you put down for that category should reflect
that individual's effect on your anxiety level. For example, if
you have one parent or one sibling or one friend who makes
you particularly anxious, your score for that category should
reflect that person's influence and not an average that
includes all others in the category.

Analyzing Your Answers

The first three questions focus on results: the results you've gotten, the results you want, and the difference between the two.
On a very basic level, anxiety equals the gap between reality and
expectations. The further your reality is from your expectations,
the more anxious you may feel. Pointing this out is by no means
intended to discourage you from setting your sights high. With
determination and good preparation, scores routinely go up by
hundreds of points, and there are major rewards that go well
beyond getting a great score. But you have to know what you're
up against.

Depending on where you start, improvements of less than two hundred points should not be very difficult to achieve with regular practice, and improvements of between two hundred and four hundred points are also not uncommon. To improve by more than four hundred points—while also possible—will probably require that you truly devote yourself to this process.

Everything you've done so far in this book will help to improve your confidence and to reduce your anxiety. The next chapters will also give you specific strategies and skills for each section of the test. You can close the gap between the results you've gotten and the results you want by working at the various skills and then taking practice tests. We recommend that you take practice tests in the book *The Official SAT Study Guide: For the New SAT*. (A publication of the College Board, the makers of the SAT, this is the only book that contains practice tests made by the people who make the actual tests.) Seeing your scores go up on practice tests will have a very positive effect on anxiety.

Questions 4 and 5 examine your inner landscape. For question 4, count the checks you marked for a, b, c, d, e, g, i, and j. Subtract the number of checks for f and h. Write your total: _____ .

Question 4: How You Handle Setbacks

Your score	Analysis
−2 – 0	Very cool
1 – 2	Cool
3 – 4	Anxious
5 – 6	Very anxious
7 – 8	Severely anxious

Given the nature of this test, with problems that demand real-time thinking, you can expect to find questions that, at least initially, look impossible. It's an inherently stressful situation. If you're used to staying calm and mentally present when faced with difficult challenges, you have an advantage. This is an area, however, where most people need work.

You may be surprised to discover, for instance, that not caring (answer choice c) and never failing (answer choice j) actually increase anxiety. When you don't care, you've given up. The act of giving up, of surrendering, always feels, at least at first, like a relief. In many situations, quitting *is* a huge relief. When you quit worrying about your fantasy baseball team that can't seem to win or when you quit trying to win the heart of someone who's incapable of appreciating you, these are good things. But when you stop caring about something that you know means a lot to you, you may experience a keen sense of loss. This can leave you carrying around a big lump of anxiety in your gut. So can never failing.

If you've never experienced a setback in school, the challenges of the SAT may take you into new territory. It probably means you're used to controlling the outcome of tests by studying hard so that you can anticipate every question. You are certainly intelligent, but you can never feel sure of your own intelligence. Take your brain out for a test drive. Try doing a practice test and notice where you get stuck and how you handle those moments. This test offers you the opportunity to work on *how* you think. Working on your mental approach to the test can make a huge difference in your score while also helping you relax and trust your abilities more.

For question 5, add up the numbers next to answer choices a, b, d, f, g, and h and write down your total: _____ . Now add up the numbers next to answer choices c and e. Subtract the second total from the first and write down your result: _____ .

Question 5: Your Inner Boss

Your score	Analysis
<1	Very positive
1-2	Okay
3-5	Annoying
6+	It's a miracle you don't quit.

Question 5 invites you to look at what goes on in your head. Imagine working for a boss who is constantly whining and insulting you. "Why can't you go any faster?" "You're such an idiot." "Oh, great. You blew it again." At first you may feel motivated to want to impress this boss. You may work extra hard to make him or her see your worth. But after a while, if the tone didn't change, you'd stop trying. The right thing to do in that situation is to quit and get a different job.

Now what if that boss lives in your head? What a drag! Every time you try to do something, you're waiting for the putdown to come. This is especially significant on the SAT, where you have to try new things all the time to find answers for the quirky questions.

More on this below, but here's the first step toward improving your inner boss: become aware of her/him. What are you saying to yourself? What are the words and how are you saying them? What's the tone? Is there ever any positive feedback?

Awareness can make a huge difference. Most of us don't notice how harsh we're being with ourselves. Noticing it can immediately begin to blunt the impact by taking us a step away from the harshness. If you're paying attention, you can't help noticing how wrong or even ridiculous these criticisms seem. You're not a moron because you can't follow a tricky math question. Your life's not hopeless because you can't remember whether the word *indigent* means "poor" or "local." To notice these thoughts is to begin to see them for what they are. With practice and awareness, you can train yourself to have a more reasonable and productive inner boss.

For question 6, write down the highest number you wrote (i.e., if "Friends" got a 7, "Siblings" got a 6, and "Parent(s)" got a 3, write down 7). Multiply that high number by the number of categories for which you scored above a 5. In other words, if "Parent(s)" got an 8, but both of the other categories were 5 or lower, you would just multiply the 8 by 1 and get 8. If another one of the other categories was also above 5, you'd multiply the 8 by 2 to get 16, and if both other categories were 6 or higher, you'd multiply the 8 by 3 and get 24. Write your result: _____ .

Question 6: External Pressures

Your score	Analysis
1-5	No sweat
6-7	A drag, but manageable
8-15	You have to address this.
16-21	A serious challenge—get help.
22-30	Call 911.

This question addresses external causes of anxiety. Family and friends can generate a great deal of anxiety around the SAT. First of all, they may not understand the test. Parents also aren't the ones taking the test and so cannot control the outcome. This makes them anxious, and they can pass that anxiety along to you. In preparation to take the SAT, one student, Sam, came in to New York City from Connecticut every weekend for tutoring. Soon after the tutoring began, his tutor asked Sam to start taking practice tests each week on his own, which they would score together during their tutoring sessions. The first practice test was a huge success. Sam's score went up over 250 points from his PSAT. But on each of the next two practice tests, Sam's score dropped a hundred points.

It turned out that as soon as his parents picked him up after each tutoring session, their first question was "What'd you get on your practice test?" Anyone can understand why they'd want to know, but the effect on Sam was terrible. By asking him right away, his parents passed their anxieties onto Sam. As soon as they stopped asking, Sam's scores shot right back up, and he ended up exceeding his goals on the real test.

Another student, Melissa, felt stuck. She had been practicing for months, but she couldn't manage to get much above 650 on any section. Most students would love to have such a problem, but she felt these were mediocre scores. Melissa was a straight-A student with fives on several AP tests. Often when she made mistakes on SAT questions, Melissa would say something like, "Oh, I'm so stupid" and laugh nervously. Her tutor pointed out to her that she was obviously not stupid and asked her why she kept saying she was. Melissa would just shrug. After two or three weeks with little change and more and more "I'm stupid" comments, the tutor changed the question. "Who told you that you were stupid?" he asked. This time, Melissa really thought about it. She realized that in her family she had a reputation for being absent-minded—forgetting her keys, losing money, stuff like that. No big deal. Her older brother, however, teased her relentlessly about it, constantly calling her stupid, and no one disagreed. Maybe he was just kidding around, but coming from an older brother, these words had a profound impact.

The next time he said it, Melissa changed the script. She clarified for him that while she might at times be absent-minded, she was definitely not stupid and had the grades to prove it. Her brother apologized, and Melissa went on to score two 800s and a 700 on her SAT.

14
Anxiety Examples

Anxiety Scenario #1: The Blank-Out

The big day finally arrives. You've prepared carefully, taken many practice tests, and memorized hundreds of SAT words. The proctor finishes reading the instructions and tells you to begin the first section. Perhaps your heart is racing and your mouth is dry, or perhaps you have no outward physical symptoms.

You open the test booklet, read the first question, and... nothing. It might as well be written in Old Norse. You are reading the words, but you have no idea what they mean. You try the second question. Same result. You try the third, the fourth—no luck. Now you feel the blood rushing to your face and your temples. Your heart is in your throat. It may be a familiar feeling or one you've experienced only in nightmares. The fear is pouring into your body like water into a leaky boat. You're sunk.

Solution: When this happened to Jesse, one of Matt's students, he started to panic. Jesse was a very strong math student and had never had trouble with the easier questions at the beginning of each Math section. Because he was used to the idea of skipping and coming back, however, Jesse's automatic response was a good one. He didn't waste time struggling. Instead, he simply kept skipping until he found his panic dying down. Unfortunately, this didn't happen until number ten. But Jesse held his form. He calmly went back and answered all the questions he had skipped. He ended up with a 750 on the Math section that day.

Anxiety Scenario #2: The Loaf of Bread

Remember those standardized tests you took when you were a little kid? I (Susan) remember taking the California Test of Basic Skills as an elementary school student. The example question at the beginning of the first section had the image of a loaf of bread. It looked so homey and inviting. All you had to do was circle the right word for this nice picture. The first questions on the test were always easy, too. You cruised through them feeling great. "What was I so worried about?" you asked yourself, relieved. "This test is a piece of cake!" (or a slice of bread). Then you got to some question in the middle of the test, or maybe even toward the end, and you felt yourself start to deflate. You read the question over and over. You wanted to cry or pound your fists. You wanted to walk out of the room.

Solution: As we mentioned at the outset, how you handle the mental wall that goes up in your mind when you confront a tricky SAT question will determine how well you perform. To succeed, you will have to use all your resources. For starters, you must skip and come back in a timely fashion, before fears and anxieties overwhelm your ability to read and think. Most important, when you come back to such a question, you will want to actually read it again. Nine times out of ten, a question appears hard because you have misread or misunderstood it. (The next section will address reading in more detail.) Read the question again with beginner's mind, open only to the words on the page, while letting go of other, extraneous thoughts. Remind yourself that the present moment is only about reading and understanding these words and that you have all the knowledge and ability within yourself to understand and succeed.

Anxiety Scenario #3: The Undertow

"Wait, was that answer right?" you ask yourself. You've just answered the question, but... maybe you're being too hasty. You read it over, and, as you do, you start to contemplate a hundred different aspects of the question that you didn't notice before. You hesitate. You want to move on. There are so many more problems, but you don't want to get this one wrong. You linger around the question, inventing dozens of ways to interpret what it means. Like the undertow at the beach, your doubts pull you back into the question, tossing you into waves of confusion. "No, I didn't have the right answer," you tell yourself. And now you have no idea how you'll find it.

Solution: The solution to the undertow is not to give in to it. Instead of going right back into answers you suspect might be wrong, mark them and come back after you've done a few more questions. A fresh look at the question will allow you to see the mistake, if you've made one, or reaffirm your answer if it was right.

Anxiety Scenario #4: The Flibber Hesitation Syndrome

You're not anxious at all. You don't mind taking this test. No big deal. You understand all of the questions, ah...somewhat. Well, actually, a lot of the questions are kind of tough. You hesitate for a moment; you don't like it. You don't like hesitating at all, because, well, it's not a good feeling to be just hesitating. So you flibber-flab. I mean, you put down an answer...decisively... sort of.

Somewhere in the back of your mind, you know that you won't be happy when you get the result. It's gonna hurt, but that day's a long way off. Who knows? If you're lucky, maybe you even got a bunch of questions right! (And maybe you've just won the lottery, too.)

Solution: The Flibber Hesitation Syndrome (don't look for it in a psych textbook; we made it up) is the hardest form of anxiety to tackle. In order to improve, you will first have to acknowledge how anxious the test is making you. You will probably have to improve your reading level (see reading chapters), and you will have to start taking a stand by answering only the questions you truly understand. On the other hand, if you are willing to stop guessing and start reading, your score can go up by hundreds of points.

Anxiety Scenario #5: The Endgamer

You once got a nearly perfect score on a practice test. That was the good news. Unfortunately, it's been all downhill from there. Since that day, every time you take a practice test, you can't help thinking about that high score. You start to do well, get excited, and then make careless errors in bunches. It's gotten to the point where, like Hamlet, you don't even want to try.

You are endgaming: playing the game for the outcome instead of just playing the game.

Solution: You must train yourself to focus on the present moment. You are perfectly capable of achieving the score you want. You've proved it. But in order to achieve it again, you will have to stop thinking about achieving it. Meditation and a meditative approach to the test can get you used to focusing only on the questions.

Anxiety Scenario #6: Monkey Mind

Whenever you sit down to do a practice test, all your thoughts get jumbled up. Your mind leaps from one thought to the next, and you find it hard to stay focused on anything at all. You read and reread questions and find that you can't even begin to say what they were about. It's as if you are reading without understanding anything. You are really worried that even on the real thing—the actual SAT—you won't be able to settle your mind down and focus on the questions.

Sometimes this same thing happens when you are lying in bed at night and start to think about all that you have to do.

Your mind starts to race, and even though you are exhausted, soothing sleep is the last thing that's going to happen.

Solution: Like the Endgamer, you too must focus on the present moment. Start using the breathing and meditation strategies to calm your mind down. Practice these strategies when you are lying in bed at night, suffering from insomnia. Practice them when you are doing test prep. During the actual SAT, you won't have time to meditate, although you can take deep breaths and be mindful of your breathing and your body. Before the test and during the breaks, you can do these exercises. If you improve your focus and concentration during practice tests, it's likely that you will be able to benefit from this work on the actual SAT. Also, make sure that you have prepared well; then you can be confident that you are ready to do your best on the test.

IV

Reading

The dear good people don't know how long it takes to learn to read.
I've been at it eighty years, and can't say yet that I've reached the goal.

—Wolfgang von Goethe

15
Reading Challenges

The biggest obstacles to succeeding on the SAT have to do with reading. For the SAT you have to read accurately and understand what you read. That may sound simple, but most of us don't do it.

Try reading the following:

The pink cat chased the orange mouse.

That was easy. You read it and understood it. It happens to be nonsense, but you have no trouble understanding what it means. You may even have a weird image in your head.

Now try this:

Karoomscheck bresheth gimmelstob velleity sharvool karma bouganvillea.

Did you get through it? Some nonsense is easier to read than other nonsense. Even though you know how to read, it's hard to keep sounding words out when you don't understand what they mean and when the combinations of letters are unfamiliar.

Now try this:

> **Failing to hide his outrage, Charles insisted that even the most ardent neoconservative pundits must acknowledge that it would take a prestidigitator to extricate us from our nation's latest boondoggle on foreign soil.**

If you can read that sentence through once and understand every word, you should put this book down. You won't need it or any other book to help you prepare for the SAT. Stop worrying and go take the test.

For the rest of us, this is an extreme example of the kind of challenge we might face on a difficult SAT question. For most people, the phrase "ardent neoconservative pundits" will slow the pace considerably. If that doesn't do it, the word "prestidigitator" looms like a brick wall two-thirds of the way through the sentence.

Even if you happen to know what these words mean, this is not the kind of sentence you can read and understand quickly. When we read difficult material, we don't take the information in the way a bar-code scanner reads a price. We may understand some parts and miss others completely. We also have to figure out all the relationships among the different parts of the sentence. For many of us, whether we sound out the words accurately or not, the sentence will come across more like this:

Failing to hide his outrage, Charles insisted that even the most ardent neo-blah blah must acknowledge that it would take a blah, blah, blah to blah blah us from our nation's latest blah blah blah on foreign soil.

Figuring this sentence out demands persistence. If you are a confident, experienced reader, you might understand about 85 percent of the words the first time through. Unfortunately, the 15 percent that you don't get can mean 0 percent comprehension of the whole thing.

On the SAT, missing a couple of words may mean you can't get the right answer. If you're a confident reader, you won't give in to the initial panic you might feel when you first encounter a difficult word or phrase. You'll reread or skip and come back and work your way into the meaning of the sentence. You'll figure out what you need to know and solve the problem.

But not everyone's a confident reader.

A student who's a news junkie and happens to know what "neoconservative pundits" are has an advantage here, but even that student may get stopped by the word "prestidigitator." Many people don't know some of the words in this sentence and might only sense that Charles was angry about something that had to do with politics—or something like that.

How does it feel to read something you can't understand? Do you feel angry? Panicked? Frustrated? Do you want to give up? All of these are natural responses, but they won't help you get the right answer. We're all human, and feeling as though we're going to fail has a powerful effect on us. We would be foolish to ignore that effect or pretend it's not happening.

That's where skipping and coming back comes in. On the SAT, you must expect that at some point you will find a question that you simply don't understand at first. You may say, "Well, when that happens, I'll just keep reading it until it makes sense." And if you can stay calm while doing that, it may work.

But most of us don't stay calm when reading something we don't understand—especially on a timed test. If we try to force ourselves to concentrate and read it again right away, we end up battling both the words on the page and our own frustration.

Skipping and coming back allows the frustrations to die down, so that when you return to the question your mind can focus only on the words.

Let's revisit that sentence:

Failing to hide his outrage, Charles insisted that even the most ardent neoconservative pundits must acknowledge that it would take a prestidigitator to extricate us from our nation's latest boondoggle on foreign soil.

On the second visit, you should find yourself less alarmed or startled. You may even discover that some parts of the sentence are coming into focus. Start with the parts you understand:

Failing to hide his outrage...

That means he was angry, and he showed it.

Charles insisted that even the most...

If you think about it, you may notice that you don't need to know the exact definition of "ardent neoconservative pundits." Charles is angry, and he disagrees with the perspective of a particular group of people. That phrase describes the people he disagrees with.

Failing to hide his outrage, Charles insisted that even the [people Charles disagrees with] must acknowledge that it would take a . . .

Okay, let's assume we don't know and have no hope of figuring out what a "prestidigitator" is. Focus elsewhere. The word you really need to know is the next word—"extricate." If you don't know what it means, you should skip this question. If you know that it means "remove from complication; liberate," then you will also quickly assume that a prestidigitator is someone who liberates. So now we have:

Failing to hide his outrage, Charles insisted that even the [people Charles disagrees with] must acknowledge that it would take a [person who can extricate] to extricate us from our nation's latest [something] on foreign soil.

Charles is angry with this group of people, with whom he strongly disagrees, and believes that even they should admit that something our country is doing overseas is bad.

Obviously, knowing that "neoconservative pundits" are those people you see on TV talking about politics (and generally favoring Republican policies) and that a "prestidigitator" is a magician and that a "boondoggle" is an unnecessary (and usually wasteful) project would make reading and understanding this sentence a lot easier. Even knowing one or two of those words would help.

But while knowing those words may help on this question, *a patient, confident approach* to reading will help on *every* question. How many high school students know what "ardent neoconservative pundits," "prestidigitator," *and* "boondoggle" mean? Not many. Ask around. See if you can find even one. Any student who can read and who is patient can go through the reading process described here and come up with the basic gist of the sentence.

The test makers know this. They don't expect you to know every word in the English language (though it certainly wouldn't hurt to learn a lot of new words). But if you can read thoughtfully, allowing your mind to build from the parts you understand, you can get what you need to do the test.

16

Reading Habits That Get in the Way and How to Correct Them

If you don't like to read very much, maybe there's a reason. Maybe reading isn't comfortable for you. Students who say that they read only what's assigned for school and tend to stay away from doing any reading on their own may have one of two issues:

- They may have poor decoding skills.
- They may transpose, change, or exclude words as they read.

"Poor decoding skills" means that when you come to an unfamiliar word, you don't sound it out. If you don't sound out words like *surreptitious, synagogue,* or *consternation*—and instead skip over them—this may be your issue. If when you're reading a book for school, you don't bother to sound out the foreign-sounding last names of the characters and almost instinctively avoid them, you should probably take a look at your decoding skills.

Decoding means just what it sounds like—deciphering the code: taking in the letters on the page and translating them in your mind into their corresponding sounds.

Of course, if you've made it to high school and are reading this book, you're able to decode. You can probably read and understand most of what you read. For the SAT, however, you may need to be a more confident reader than you already are. There are a fair number of big words on the SAT, and you'll want to decode *and* understand most of them.

Like walking or talking, reading is a developmental skill. Some babies learn to talk at eight or nine months. Many others say their first words at about a year. Some babies reach eighteen months without saying a single word. Albert Einstein didn't start talking until he was four years old. In the end, almost every baby winds up talking—it's just a matter of when.

The same is true of reading. Some kids learn to read at two or three. Most learn to read in first grade. Many kids struggle with reading and don't become fluent readers until second or third grade. Just as many one-year-olds lack the motor or thinking skills they need to talk, not every six-year-old brain is ready to learn how to read.

You would never label a child who doesn't talk at fifteen or sixteen months a "late talker." But almost every boy and girl is expected to read in the first grade. By the end of first grade, if you're still not reading, you start to feel left behind. You may try so hard to read that you end up memorizing the shapes of hundreds of words. It's a lot harder than sounding words out, but if you can't follow the letters and words across the page, you do what you have to do. It's what learning specialists call "compensating."

As you get older, of course, your brain catches up. If we all learned to read in fifth grade instead of first, there might not be "late readers." But if you're not reading confidently by, say, second grade, chances are that you may develop habits that let you get by without ever addressing your basic difficulties. You may get in the habit of reading only the words that come easily and skipping over the bigger, more unfamiliar words.

Not decoding confidently takes a lot of the fun out of reading. It's fine if you're reading something basic, but when you read something that's full of words you don't recognize, you can't enjoy it or get much from it.

Fortunately, there's a solution: teach yourself to decode! When you come to a big word, instead of skipping over it, get in the habit of sounding it out. Say each syllable to yourself, one at a time. Then put all the syllables back together as a word. (You can also get the dictionary to help you: use the pronunciation guide and read the definitions. Become confident about how to pronounce new words and learn what they mean.)

You may feel silly doing this at first. This is something little kids do! But maybe you didn't get to do it when you were little. Or, if you did, maybe it was too much of a struggle at the time. Now it won't be. Go back to the basics, and you'll find that with a little practice it gets easier and easier. Often the words you haven't been reading are words you'd recognize in conversation.

So sounding them out makes all the difference. Before you know it, you may even enjoy reading.

The other common reading issue, which makes the SAT difficult for many students, is what some call "the jumpy eye." If you have a jumpy eye, you don't always read every word in the order that it's written or exactly as it's written on the page. You may leave a word out or transpose a word from the line above or below, or you may change a word, replacing it with one that sounds better in your head (and seemingly makes sense). None of this is done on purpose. We've heard students who do this berate themselves for being lazy, but that's not accurate either.

The truth is that having a jumpy eye is part of life. Everyone has it to one extent or another. Our focus tends to jump around, especially when we're under pressure and reading something difficult. The challenge is to become self-aware enough to notice, accept reality, and allow your focus to return as many times as necessary until the meaning becomes clear.

If your reading eye tends to jump a lot, you've probably experienced some frustration as a reader, and the SAT may feel overwhelming. In fact, the SAT is an excellent opportunity for you. Your habits have left you wary of reading, and your fears about the SAT are well founded, but the good news is that you can improve your reading skills.

Brian was a B+/A– student at an excellent school. He was thoughtful, well spoken, and well liked, and he could play the clarinet like Lance Armstrong rides a bike—with passion, intensity, and great skill. But Brian scored in the mid-50s on all three sections of the PSAT, while many of his friends scored in the high 60s and 70s. Making matters worse, Brian's older sister, Phoebe, had gotten high scores on all her standardized tests and was accepted by every school to which she applied—MIT, Harvard, and Yale. Brian felt anxious and hopeless about taking the SAT. He had no idea how he could possibly improve.

He also had no idea how jumpy his reading eye was. For Brian, an SAT question like "If the ratio of x to y is 7 to 5, what will the value of x be when y is 5,000,000?" read as: "If the ratio of x to y is 7 to 5, what will the *ratio* of x be when y is 5,000,000?" You'll notice that, if you read the question accurately, it's not too hard. But when Brian substituted the word "ratio" for "value" in the second part of the question, it became impossible. It's a *tiny* mistake. What's the big deal? It's just *one* little word. The changed version even sounds like an SAT question. But that one tiny change makes getting the right answer to the real question impossible.

When he started studying for the SAT, Brian did not realize how far off his initial take on things often was. It didn't occur to him that there was any issue at all with reading. Brian loved to read. He read books and newspaper stories and magazine articles and understood them pretty well for a seventeen-year-old. He didn't notice whether there were words or phrases or even paragraphs that gave him difficulty. He was, after all, intelligent—people with jumpy eyes often are. He managed to understand the gist of what he read without getting a lot of the particulars.

As soon as Brian understood the way his mind scrambled up

some questions, he began to work on this. He quickly realized that in order to understand every word and the relationships among words within sentences, he would need to read even easy questions more than once. In fact, the first reading for Brian served as an introduction or preview for finding out what the sentence was about. On the third or fourth reading, he began to pull together all the details.

You may think this process will take too long, but imagine how much time you might spend trying and failing to do a problem after reading it as Brian did.

Brian learned to work efficiently and accurately. He ended up with a 770 on the Verbal (what's now called Critical Reading) and a 720 on the Math. He also slew a lot of demons along the way. He learned to focus his attention and manage his jumpy way of reading so that he could feel confident about his abilities in any situation.

17
Reading Assessment

Reading comprehension is like the motor of a car—if every part functions well and the motor is put together properly, the motor as a whole will function well, but even when some of the parts are not functioning very well, the motor sometimes still runs, albeit poorly.

—*The Cognitive Elements of Reading*

As you already know from the earlier chapters on reading, to do well on all sections of the SAT you must be a strong reader. In other words, all parts of your motor must be running well, particularly because every question requires skillful reading and because the reading level of the test is high. What may also be challenging is that you may not be interested in what you have to read on the test. In general, we tend to read better when we are interested in the content. In reading something that doesn't interest you, you face a major challenge to your focus and concentration.

The questions below ask you to reflect on what sort of reader you are. At the heart of Zen is the process of watching and noticing, which is what you will do now in order to understand yourself as a reader. Being aware of your reading habits and skills will enable you to determine where you most need to focus as you prepare for the SAT, as well as what you can do to become a better reader in general. You can determine specific ways to improve your reading skills based on what sort of reader you are. If you aren't already a close, careful reader, perhaps you are ready to become one.

1. When you have some time to yourself, how do you choose to spend it? Rank the following activities from 8 down to 1 (with 8 as your favorite and 1 as your least favorite):

   _____ Exercising / working out
   _____ Hanging out with friends
   _____ Playing video games
   _____ Listening to music
   _____ Watching movies (either in the theater or at home)
   _____ Reading
   _____ Cleaning
   _____ Cooking

2. If you *had* to pick from the following list, which would you choose to read?

a. Jane Austen's *Pride and Prejudice*

b. *Teen People*

c. *Sports Illustrated*

d. A serious newspaper (*New York Times, Wall Street Journal, Washington Post, Los Angeles Times*)

e. A more entertainment-oriented newspaper (*USA Today* or tabloid)

f. The back of your favorite CD case

g. *Scientific American*

h. A weekly news magazine (*Time, Newsweek, U.S. News & World Report*)

i. Nothing

3. How often do you read something that wasn't assigned in school?

a. Every day

b. Twice a week

c. Once a week

d. Once a month

e. Almost never

f. Never

4. How much reading goes on in your home? Do members of your family read?

a. All the time

b. Often

    c. Sometimes

    d. Once in a while

    e. Almost never

    f. Never

5. How long can you stay focused when you read?

    a. Not long (under fifteen minutes)

    b. Thirty minutes to an hour

    c. An hour or two

    d. Hours

6. Do you consider yourself to be

    a. a fast reader?

    b. an average-paced reader?

    c. a slow reader?

7. In the passage below from Nathaniel Hawthorne's *The Scarlet Letter*, how many words would you be unable to define? (Include any words that you can't define regardless of whether you have seen or heard them before.)

The founders of a new colony, whatever Utopia of human virtue and happiness they might originally project, have invariably recognized it among their earliest practical necessities to allot a portion of the virgin soil as a cemetery, and another portion as the site of a prison. In accordance with this rule, it may safely be assumed that the forefathers of Boston had built the first prison-house, somewhere in the vicinity of Cornhill, almost as seasonably as they marked out the first burial-ground, on Isaac Johnson's lot, and round about his grave, which subsequently became the nucleus of all the congregated sepulchres in the old churchyard of King's Chapel. Certain it is, that, some fifteen or twenty years after the settlement of the town, the wooden jail was already marked with weather-stains and other indications of age, which gave a yet darker aspect to its beetle-browed and gloomy front. The rust on the ponderous ironwork of its oaken door looked more antique than any thing else in the new world. Like all that pertains to crime, it seemed never to have known a youthful era. Before this ugly edifice, and between it and the wheel-track of the street, was a grass-plot, much overgrown with burdock, pig-weed, apple-peru, and such unsightly vegetation, which evidently found something congenial in the soil that had so early borne the black flower of civilized society, a prison. But, on one side of the portal, and rooted almost at the threshold, was a wild rose-bush, covered, in this month of June, with its delicate gems, which might be imagined to offer their fragrance and fragile beauty to the prisoner as he went in, and to the condemned criminal as he came forth to his doom, in token that the deep heart of Nature could pity and be kind to him.

a. 12 or more words
b. 9–11 words
c. 5–8 words
d. 0–4 words

8. Read the sentence below twice and then pick the response that best describes your experience reading it.

Calliope, the muse of epic poetry, brought a plethora of inspiration and perspicacity to poets everywhere, whose poetry was sometimes in an inchoate condition, and so her magnanimous attention was warmly welcomed.

   a. I read the sentence easily and had little trouble with any of the words in it.
   b. I read the sentence easily and generally understood what it meant, even though I don't really know the definitions of a lot of the words.
   c. I read the sentence easily even though I have no idea what it means.
   d. I stumbled over a few of the big words but was able to pronounce them, and when I read it again, I read more confidently.
   e. I didn't know most of the big words but tried to pronounce them. It was still hard for me when I read it again.
   f. It would take too much effort to sound out so many big words, and I wouldn't understand it anyway.

9. When you are reading and come across words you don't know, what do you do?

    a. Skip them.

    b. Look them up in the dictionary.

    c. Try to figure them out from how they are used.

Understanding Your Assessment

The first six questions focus on your reading habits. Almost all test preparation materials tell kids to read a lot because the SAT is fundamentally a reading test. Whether you are wrapping your mind around complicated sentences in the Math section or making your way through a reading passage, your reading skills will be taxed. Reading a lot—beyond what is assigned in school—is an important way to develop your reading skills. However, *what* you read and *how* you read are also critical.

1. The first question is pretty obvious. Reading doesn't have to be your favorite activity, but if it ranked at the bottom of your list, below, say, cleaning, you should probably start figuring out what's wrong. Your score for this question is the ranking you assigned reading.

                             Write your score here: ____

2. Use the following chart to determine what score to give yourself for the second question:

Answer Choice(s)	Score
i	0
b or f	1
c or e	2
a or h	3
d	4
g	5

   Write your score here: _____

   If you scored a 2 or lower on this question, you can probably
   improve your SAT score dramatically by improving your
   reading level. See Chapter 18 for details on how to take on
   this crucial challenge. Scores of 3 or 4 indicate a good founda-
   tion, and a 5 means that you read on an extremely sophisticated level and will probably find the reading on the SAT
   very manageable.

3. Use the following chart to determine what score to give yourself for the third question:

Answer Choice	Score
a	5
b	4
c	3
d	2
e	1
f	0

4. Use the following chart to determine what score to give yourself for the fourth question:

Answer Choice	Score
a	5
b	4
c	3
d	2
e	1
f	0

   Write your total from these two questions (0 to 10) here: ____

5. Use the following chart to determine what score to give yourself for the fifth question:

Answer Choice	Score
a	1
b	3
c	5
d	6

   Write your score here: ____

6. Give yourself 2 points for being a fast reader and 3 for being
   average or slow. Slow readers tend to do better on the SAT
   where accuracy counts for a lot more than speed.

   Write your score here: ____

   Add up your total points for questions 1 through 6: ____

Use the following chart to analyze your total score for questions 1 through 6:

Score Range	Analysis
4–9	Get to work! Read Chapters 15, 16, and 18 for specific ideas about how to improve.
10–15	Plenty of room to improve. Challenging yourself in this area will yield dramatic results.
16–20	You're a solid reader. Now challenge yourself. Read op-eds and other materials that will raise your reading level.
21–25	You are a strong reader. Make sure to read Chapter 19. You can also improve by reading materials in such areas as science or personal narrative, which may challenge you.
26–32	Reading is not your issue. You should still follow the guidelines in Chapter 19 and aim to get all the reading questions right.

7. Although the SAT no longer has the Analogies section, you still need a sophisticated vocabulary to do well on the test. The level of the vocabulary is high throughout the test and especially so in the Critical Reading section.

If there were seven or more words you didn't know in the excerpt from *The Scarlet Letter*, you should build your vocabulary. If what you need is just a bigger vocabulary, then make or buy some flash cards right away. Use the vocabulary list in the appendix as a starting place. Learn all the words there. You can, of course, do more, and there are various SAT vocabulary books you can get. Additionally, look up words that you don't know when you read, and make flash cards for them. On one side of the card, write the word; on the other, the definition, the part of speech, and an example of how the word is used. Go over your cards all the time—on the bus, at the dentist's office, during breakfast. Whenever you have five minutes, go over your flash cards. Get your friends and family to quiz you. Expanding your vocabulary will make you a better reader and writer and give you a new way to relate to and think about life.

8. If you found yourself struggling to get through the excerpt from *The Scarlet Letter* and if you had difficulty reading the sentence in question 8 aloud, you may have to work on your decoding skills. If you often skip hard words, it's probably worthwhile to try to figure out why. It may be that you have to build your vocabulary, but it may be more than that. See Chapter 16 for more details. You can talk with your English teacher or the learning specialist in your school if you suspect that your struggles with polysyllabic words (words with many syllables) are bigger than just having to build your vocabulary.

9. If you answered a, you should consider whether or not you have difficulty with decoding (see Chapter 16). If you answered c, you may want to work on switching that over to b. SAT preparation is an excellent time to build your vocabulary, and most of what you read will contain vocabulary words that will be good to know beyond the test.

18

How to Raise Your Reading Level

For some people, a lack of interest in reading has nothing to do with any particular difficulty with reading itself—it's more just a lack of interest in reading. But if you don't like to read and now you want to excel on the SAT, you've got a challenge. To do well, you will have to read and understand passages about anything from how a violin is made to the experiences of Asian immigrants and the stories of a farmer from a hundred years ago. You'll have to detect when a writer is being sarcastic or ironic. In short, if you're not used to reading on a fairly sophisticated level, there's a limit to how well you can do on the SAT.

Perhaps there's a reason you don't like to read very much. (See Chapters 15, "Reading Challenges," and 16, "Reading Habits.") But whether there is or not, now's the time to become a good reader. Reading on a higher level can transform your life for the better. It will give you access to worlds you hardly know exist. You will gain a deeper appreciation for life.

Here's a simple way to raise your reading level in a fairly short amount of time: start reading newspaper editorials. In school most of the reading you do that's not from a textbook is fiction. In English class you typically read novels, short stories, plays, and poems. While the new SAT includes some fiction passages, the vast majority of reading passages are nonfiction. (Fiction means made-up stories, and nonfiction refers to all other types of writing—opinion essays; descriptions of real-life events, experiments, or situations; historical accounts; personal experiences; and anything else that's not made up.)

If you're not familiar with newspapers, the editorials are opinion articles written by the newspaper staff. While most of the paper attempts to present information in a factual and unbiased manner, editorials offer opinions. You will also want to look at op-ed articles (short for "opposite editorial"). These articles are traditionally found on the page facing the editorial page. The difference between editorials and op-eds is that editorials present the views of the newspaper staff and op-eds present the opinions of individuals on particular subjects. For example, a scientist might write an op-ed about genetic research. A teacher might write about changes in the way math is taught. A rock star might write about trends in music, or an accountant might write about changes in the tax laws. As you can see, there's a lot of variety in the op-ed section.

Reading editorials and op-eds is an ideal way to get better at understanding all kinds of nonfiction articles, and you'll learn a lot of interesting stuff doing it as well.

If you don't know where they are in the newspaper, have a

parent or teacher help you find the editorials and op-eds. Start reading them every day. At first you may not want to read the more difficult ones. That's fine. Just get started. Once you get comfortable, you can start challenging yourself with the harder pieces.

Keep a log of your reading, a notebook where you answer three questions about each article you read:

What is the article about?
What is the tone?
How is the article organized?

Your answers should be short—anything from a few words to several short sentences, at the most. For the first question, be as general as possible: "The article was about oil prices," or "cloning" or "vegetarianism." Don't get into an elaborate explanation. Work on focusing your answer as much as possible.

The second question can have a one-word answer: factual, angry, funny, cautionary.

For the third question, you'll have to look at how the article is put together. Does the author start by telling a personal story or a funny anecdote, or does she jump right into the facts of the matter? Does he list a lot of facts or mostly just offer opinions? Are there shifts in tone—from joking to serious or from factual to opinionated? You'll want to start noticing not just what words and sentences and paragraphs *mean*, but also what *functions they serve*. Doing this exercise can be rewarding on many levels. You may find that this kind of reading, beyond improving your scores, makes you more confident in general and more comfortable in the world because you will expand what you know about such things as politics, history, and social issues.

If you can't get to the newspaper every day, just make sure you read it two or three times a week. Reading editorials and op-eds intensely for a week or two will not be as beneficial as reading two or three a week for six to eight weeks or longer. You will not agree with everything you read, but there's a lot to be gained from understanding other perspectives—particularly when they're presented in good, persuasive writing. But, most important, by reading editorials and op-eds, you will become a better reader.

19
Critical Reading Strategies

Here's our three-step approach to handling the reading passages on the test. Phase 1 explains how to read the passage initially, Phase 2 focuses on how to attack the questions, and Phase 3 shows you how to identify and eliminate wrong answers and helps you recognize what to look for in a right answer. What's also important to underscore is that these strategies are secondary to concentration and focus.

Phase 1: Reading

The goal of the first phase is to understand the *main idea* of the passage. If you've been doing the op-ed exercise, this part should come easily.

- Preview:

    ○ Read the italicized summary. (Right before each reading

passage is a short introduction, which often provides helpful information.)

- ○ Quickly scan the questions (*not* the answers, just the questions).

- Read:

    - ○ Read the whole passage through to find the *main idea*.

    - ○ If you're getting confused, try skipping to the end. The main idea is almost always expressed at the end.

    - ○ Avoid getting stuck in the middle. If a paragraph is difficult, skip forward or look at the first and last sentences to get the gist of the paragraph. As long as you get the main idea, you're fine. The test often doesn't ask about the most difficult details. Also, once you understand the main idea, some of the details may make more sense.

- Jot down your answers to these two questions:

    - ○ What is the main idea? (Your answer should be as short and direct as possible: *Not* "The passage discusses how federal tax dollars get distributed to the states to support programs like Medicaid and Head Start." Rather, "Efforts by the government to ease poverty.")

    - ○ How does the author feel about it? Or, in SAT language,

"The author's overall tone in this passage is best described as..."

Phase 2: Questions

If you've got the main idea, you're ready to tackle the questions. Two suggestions:

- After you read each question, before looking at any of the answer choices, go back to the passage, find the right answer, and jot it down. This strategy helps you avoid getting confused by wrong answer choices that sound right.

  - Often the test questions will direct you to particular parts of the passage; for example, "In line 18..." The line numbers are in the right margin of the passage. About 60 percent of the time the answer will be found right at the line numbers given in the test question.

  - About 35 percent of the time the answer shows up within two sentences before or after the line citation.

  - About 5 percent of the time the answer is in a different part of the passage, nowhere near the cited line numbers.

- Always skip and come back on the reading. Here's why:

  - Unlike other sections of the SAT, where the questions go from easiest to hardest, the reading questions are randomly ordered. In fact, the test makers often put a hard question first in the Critical Reading section.

○ Skipping and coming back to difficult questions is always the best way to approach them on the test.

○ As you work your way through the questions, if you're taking our suggestions, you're rereading the passage and becoming more and more familiar with it, thereby increasing the chances that you will see the right answers.

Phase 3: Answer Choices

Most students find this phase to be the most difficult. The choices often take a form you don't expect, and several sound right. The first thing you should do is quickly read through all five answer choices *without stopping to reflect on them*. This way you avoid wasting time considering a wrong answer when the right answer is waiting nearby. Once you've read through all five, go back through and do the following:

• Eliminate an answer because the choice is...

○ too harsh. If the question asks for the tone of the passage and one of the answer choices says "bitterly sarcastic," cross it off. You will not find "bitter sarcasm" on the SAT. (That's only in the real world!)

○ too extreme. Watch out for the words "always" and "never." These words make answers that may otherwise be correct wrong. No matter how *close* an answer may be, making it too extreme usually makes it wrong.

○ not in the passage. Unlike school tests, where you're asked to read between the lines and make subtle inferences, the SAT measures your *literal* understanding of the text. Do not interpret or read into it. No matter how reasonable an answer sounds to you, if it isn't mentioned in the passage, it's wrong.

○ in the passage, but not relevant to the question. Often on a difficult question, an answer that we recognize from the passage will seem appealing. But just because it's mentioned in the passage doesn't make it the right answer for this particular question. Before choosing an answer that you see in the text, *make sure it answers the question.*

• What to look for in a right answer: The right answer is often more general than you might expect. In school, you've been trained to *be specific.* Your teachers often take away points when you fail to present enough *detailed examples* as evidence for your point of view. If a question on a history test asked you to explain the role of Martin Luther King Jr. in the civil rights movement and you said, "King was a great leader," you would probably get no credit. On the SAT, "King was a great leader" can be a *right answer.* Think about it. He *was* a great leader, and this idea may very well be the *main idea* of the reading passage.

V

Some Things You Must Know

When you know a thing, to hold that you know it; and when you do not know a thing, to allow that you do not know it — this is knowledge.

—Confucius

20

The Big Ten: Grammar and Usage

In the multiple-choice questions for Identifying Sentence Errors, which are part of the Writing section, the SAT focuses on some of the most common errors in grammar and standard English usage. These are the mistakes that come up all the time in writing and speaking. After reviewing the Big Ten, you will start to notice these errors everywhere, including in the sentences on the SAT!

There are *many* pronoun errors on the test and in the world. *Three* of the Big Ten mistakes focus on pronouns.

1. Pronoun Agreement

Within a sentence, pronouns have to agree in number with the noun to which they refer. For example: "Every *student* wanted to do well on *their* SAT test."

The subject of this sentence is *student*, a singular noun; therefore, the pronoun *their*, which refers to this student's test, must also be singular:

Every *student* wanted to do well on *his* or *her* SAT test.

Often this mistake occurs because the English language doesn't have a singular unisex pronoun, and saying "his or her" or "she or he" becomes wordy and awkward.

Another common error with pronoun agreement takes place with the pronouns *everyone* and *everybody*, which are singular in form but plural in meaning. When we use either word, we are referring to a group of people. Think about the word *everyone*: "every one" or "every person." The form and the sense are different. Think also about how the word *everyone* takes a singular verb: "Everyone *was* happy." Compare this with "The people *were* happy."

If *everyone* is singular, then *their*, which is plural in form, doesn't agree. Often you will hear people say, "*Everyone* must bring *their* books to class." The correct statement would be

Everyone must bring *his* or *her* books to class.

You can also make the subject plural to avoid "his or her": "*All students* must bring *their* books." (But on the SAT, all you need to do is find the error!)

2. Pronoun Case

Pronouns come in different forms. For example, *him*, *his*, and *he* are three different third-person singular masculine pronouns. Each of these pronouns is a different case (or form), and each has a different function. *Him* is the objective case; *his* is the possessive case; and *he* is the subjective or nominative case.

Depending on the job the pronoun has to do, the case will be different. For example, if the pronoun acts as the subject of the verb, then you need the subjective/nominative case:

He is my best friend.

If the pronoun acts as the direct object of the verb or the object of a preposition, then you need the objective case:

I like *him*.
Give your money to *him*.

The possessive case is used to show possession:

The money is *his*.
This is *his* money.

The SAT will present you with pronoun case errors such as "*Him* and his friend were late for the party." The sentence should read:

He and his friend were late for the party.

The test will undoubtedly present some pronoun case errors with "me" and "I." "Me" is the *objective* case, and "I" is the *subjective/nominative* case. Many people struggle with the differences between these two pronouns.

For example, lots of people say, "*Me* and Martina are going to the party." Actually,

Martina and *I* are going to the party.

The subject in the sentence is compound: *Martina* and *I*. For a pronoun to act as the subject here, you need the subjective/ nominative case *I*.

Once you stop making this particular mistake, you may begin to think that *I* is more correct and so use it all the time—even when you need *me*. For example, "You can give your completed surveys to Martina or *I*." Just move the pronoun next to the preposition *to*, and you'll get it right.

You can give your completed surveys to *me*...
or
You can give your completed surveys to Martina or *me*.

(*Myself* sometimes also finds itself incorrectly used in the *me* position. *Myself* is a reflective pronoun and indicates that the subject *acts upon itself*. For example, "I looked at *myself* in the mirror.")

Additionally, errors with *me* and *I* sometimes show up in the following way: "My sister is taller than *me*." This sentence should read:

My sister is taller than *I*.

What you are actually saying is "My sister is taller than *I am*." We often cut off the final verb, but the pronoun still has to be the form (subjective/nominative) that can act as a subject. Just add the final verb and you'll get this one right.

3. Ambiguous Pronoun Reference

Pronoun ambiguity typically occurs when a sentence containing two people of the same gender contains a pronoun that refers to one of them. For example, "My brother told my dad that *his* wallet had been stolen." Was the brother's wallet or the dad's wallet stolen? *His* could refer to either person. You can change the *his* to *my dad's* or *my brother's*, but you end up with a repetitive sentence. Try the following:

My brother told our dad, "My wallet has been stolen."

(Again, you won't have to rewrite the sentences on the SAT but just have to identify the error. In your own writing, though, avoid pronoun ambiguity.)

4. Subject-Verb Agreement

Every sentence has to have a subject and a verb (and a complete idea). Subjects and verbs have to agree, and most of the time they do. However, there are certain conditions that can lead to trouble.

The subject often comes before the verb in English sentences, but in unusual instances the subject follows the verb. For example, "In the library, there *was* a dictionary, a thesaurus, and a lot of other reference books." The subject here is a *dictionary*, a *thesaurus,* and a *lot*—the subject is plural and comes after the verb. The sentence should read,

In the library *were* a dictionary, a thesaurus, and a lot of other reference books.

Reverse the order by putting the subject before the verb, and you'll get it right: "A dictionary, a thesaurus, and a lot of other references books *were* in the library."

Sometimes the subject and the verb don't sit next to each other, and a lot of other words come in between them. For example, "The test with its challenging questions and unusual problems *require* a lot of focus and concentration." (*Test* is the subject, not *questions* and *problems;* the verb should be *requires.*)

The *test* with its challenging questions and unusual problems *requires* a lot of focus and concentration.

Certain words seem to be plural, but they aren't. These words include such pronouns as *everyone* and *everybody,* as well as such collective nouns as *audience* and *group.* The mistake here is logical; all of these words imply a bunch of people, but their forms are singular. The adjective *every* is also singular. "Every man, woman, and child *likes* (not *like*) ice cream."

When you use *neither/nor* or *either/or,* you must be careful. With this type of sentence construction, the verb has to agree with the subject that follows the *nor* or the *or.* For example, "Neither the dog nor the *puppies have* (not *has*) been fed." (Think: "The *puppies have* not been fed.") Here's another example: "Either the students or the *teacher was* (not *were*) to blame." (Think: "The *teacher was* to blame.")

5. Verb Tense and Verb Forms

The tense of a verb tells us the time of the action of the verb. Verbs in English have three basic tenses: present, past, and future. (There are a few other refinements of these as well.) Watch out for irregular verbs, whose forms few people seem to know well.

Confusing Verb Forms

Probably the greatest confusion is with the verbs *lie* and *lay. Lie* means "to recline or to remain in a reclining position." *Lay* means "to place," as in "I *lay* the napkins on the table." You can substitute the verb *place* for *lay*: "I *place* the napkins on the table."

The three main forms (or the principal parts) of any verb are as follows:

1. the first-person singular (I), present tense;
2. the first-person singular (I), past tense; and
3. the past participle (used with other verb forms such as, "I *have lain* in bed all day"; here the past participle joins the verb *have*).

The principal parts of *lie* are *lie, lay, lain.*

I *lie* in bed.
Yesterday I *lay* in bed.
I *have lain* in bed.

The principal parts of *lay* are *lay, laid, laid.*

I *lay* the napkins on the table.

Yesterday I *laid* the napkins on the table.

I *have laid* the napkins on the table.

Tense Shifts

Another common error is an illogical tense shift within a sentence. Often the tense is consistent throughout one sentence: "I *am* happy that it *is* Saturday because I *want* to get some sleep." (All verbs here are in the present tense.) Sometimes, however, the tense will *logically* switch within the same sentence: "When I *was* a kid, I always *wanted* to stay up late; now I *want* to go to bed but *can't* because of homework." Here the verb tense logically shifts from past to present tense. The problem comes when you lose track of tenses and end up with illogical switches: "Because it *was raining* (past tense), I *want* (present tense) an umbrella." The correct sentence should be either

Because it *was raining* (past tense), I *wanted* (past tense) an umbrella.

or

Because it *is raining* (present tense), I *want* (present tense) an umbrella.

The Subjunctive

"If I were the king of the forest..." You may remember this line from one of the songs in *The Wizard of Oz*. Here the cowardly lion tells us what he would do if he *were* the king of the forest (under this particular condition). The most common instance of the subjunctive occurs with the verb *to be* and requires the *were* form to refer to something that is nonfactual or contrary to fact (the lion is NOT the king of the forest). In determining whether you need *was* or *were,* ask yourself whether you are setting up a particular condition that is not the case (almost like an imaginary *What if...*). For example,

If I *were* in charge of the SAT, I would start the test with ten minutes of meditation.

(I'm not in charge...)

6. Faulty Parallelism

You probably remember the Sesame Street song "One of These Things Is Not Like the Other." That principle is what you have to keep in mind to identify faulty parallelism errors.

When there's a list within a sentence, each item in the list—whether it's an adjective, a noun, a prepositional phrase, or something else—must take the same form. For example: "The boy was *smart, curious,* and *liked* to use the computer." The sentence presents two adjectives, but then the third item in the list is a verb. There are various ways to correct this error:

The boy was *smart* and *curious,* and *he liked* to use the computer.

or

The boy was *smart, curious,* and *savvy* about technology.

7. False or Illogical Comparisons

Sometimes we take a kind of mental shortcut, and the result is a faulty comparison. Ask yourself what is being compared. Does it make sense? Are the two things really comparable? "Martina was unhappy because *her clothes* were not as fashionable as *her friends*." Can you compare clothes to friends? That's what the structure of the sentence implies. Instead, you should compare things that are similar:

> **Martina was unhappy because *her clothes* were not as fashionable as *her friends' clothes*.**

You also need to avoid illogical comparisons. For example: "I like apples and peaches, but apples are the *best* fruit." Something can't be the best one when there are only two items being compared. With two items, you have to use the comparative (*better*) rather than the superlative (*best*).

> **I like apples and peaches, but apples are the better fruit.**

8. Adjectives and Adverbs

Adjectives modify nouns and pronouns. Adverbs modify verbs, adjectives, and other adverbs. They sometimes get confused. The trouble with adverbs and adjectives often surfaces when they are used together. For example: "Something should be done about the *rapid* increasing number of toxic waste sites in cities." *Rapid* should be an adverb, which modifies *increasing*: "*rapidly* increasing number."

Often *good* and *well* get mixed up. *Good* is an adjective and *well* is an adverb. "My friend is a good runner, and she also dances well." The exception to this is health. You can say both "I feel good today" and "I feel well today." (*Good* is for psychological well-being, and *well* is for physical well-being.) Don't say the following: "I did *good* on my grammar test." Avoid this kind of irony! Here you must use the adverb *well*:

I did *well* on my grammar test.

9. Wrong Words

There are many words that seem similar but are actually different in meaning. For example, *affect* and *effect* are often used incorrectly. There are a number of these similar but different words.

Some of the most common ones include the following:

affect / effect
aggravated / irritated
allusion / illusion
imminent / eminent
complement / compliment
conscience / conscious / conscientious
desert / dessert
its / it's
lose / loose
principal / principle
they're / their / there
your / you're

Use your dictionary to look up the words on this list so that you can be sure to use each correctly and to identify when they are used incorrectly.

10. Idioms / Wrong Prepositions

There are various idiom errors on the SAT. Most often these errors consist of wrong prepositions. Idiom has to do with the conventions of a language—the established usage. What's particularly tricky in English is that we use certain prepositions after nouns, adjectives, and verbs, but there aren't rules that govern which prepositions should be used. For example, we agree *with* another person, we agree *to* a proposal, and people may agree *upon* a plan. We get angry *at* or *about* an action but *with* a person. We get angered *by* actions. For example, "I was angered *with* your behavior at the hockey game," is wrong. The correct idiom would be, "I was angered *by* your behavior at the hockey game." Often we can identify idiom errors because they just sound wrong.

21
Math Strategies

There are two ideas that you should keep in mind at all times on the Math sections of the test:

1. Even though it's a math test, your success depends on how accurately you *read*.

2. It's often better to solve the math problems by using real numbers or real situations instead of using algebra.

Here are some words—we call them "trigger words"—that you'll want to pay special attention to on the Math sections. On the test, underline these words and use their meanings to decipher the questions:

- Integer: This means "whole number" (no fractions or decimals). Remember that 0 and negative numbers can also be integers.

- Number: Test questions usually say "integer," so when it says "number," remember to include fractions.

- Sum, product, and difference: The sum is the result in an addition problem. The product is the result in a multiplication problem. The difference is the result in a subtraction problem. Be patient with these. Make sure you sort out what each one refers to.

- Must: "Must" means no exceptions. If it says "must," look for an exception to disprove the problem.

- Could: "Could" means only one case has to work. If you find one that works, you're done.

- Least, greatest, and any other similar words such as maximum, minimum, less than, and greater than. Make sure you follow how they affect the problem.

- Digit: a single number: 0, 1, 2, 3, 4, 5, 6, 7, 8, or 9.

- Units' digit: the ones' place. (In 783, the 7 is in the hundreds' place, the 8 is in the tens' place, and 3 is the units' digit.)

- Factor: An integer that divides evenly into another; for example, the factors of 6 are 1, 2, 3, and 6.

- Multiple: The multiples of a number are all the values that result from multiplying that number by anything but 0; for example, the multiples of 6 are 6, 12, 18, 24, 30, etc.

- Prime number: a number that has exactly two positive factors, itself and 1.

- Mean: average, or the sum of a set of numbers divided by the number of elements in the set.

- Median: the middle number in a list of numbers when you line them up from smallest to biggest; for example, for the numbers 1, 2, 5, 87, and 703, the median is 5.

- Mode: the number that occurs most frequently in a set of numbers. There may be one, more than one, or no mode; for example, for the numbers 3, 7, 3, 59, 1, and 88, the mode is 3.

- Remainder: When you have divided as far as you can without using decimals, what has not been divided yet is the remainder.

- Consecutive: In order. Just watch out for tricks.

- Positive and even: For some reason, our minds tend to confuse these terms. If a question asks for "three positive, consecutive integers," be aware that 4, 6, and 8 are *not* consecutive.

- Area and perimeter: Be careful not to confuse these. The area is the amount of space in a flat object (e.g., the area of a rectangle = length × width; the area of a circle = πr^2). The perimeter is the distance around an object.

- Circumference, radius, chord, diameter: The circumference is the perimeter of a circle. A radius is any line connecting the center of a circle with its circumference. A chord is any line connecting two points on the circumference of a circle. The longest chord is the diameter, which runs through the center, has a length equal to two radii, and divides the circle into two equal semicircles.

Plugging In

Try this:

Molly goes to the store and buys x pineapples for y cents each. If she gives the clerk z dollars, how much change, in cents, will she get back from the clerk in terms of x, y, and z?

a. $\frac{z}{xy}$

b. $z - xy$

c. $xy - z$

d. $100z - xy$

e. $z - \frac{y}{x}$

Did you get it? Jot down your answer.

Now try this one:

Molly goes to the store. She buys 3 pineapples for 150 cents each. If she gives the clerk 5 dollars, how much change will she get back from the clerk?

The two questions are the same, but the second one has numbers instead of variables. Which one was easier to answer?

Most people would prefer the second version. We're all used to figuring out how much things cost.

Almost any problem where *the answer choices contain variables* can be solved by substituting real numbers. When you see variables in the answer choices, try this:

1. Choose numbers for all the variables in the problem and *write them down*. (In the problem above, we made $x = 3$, $y = 150$, and $z = 5$.)

2. Solve the problem using your numbers. (5 dollars minus 450 cents [3 times 150] equals 50 cents.)

3. Write your answer down and circle it. (50.)

4. Plug your numbers into the answer choices to see which one gives the answer you got.

The right answer to the original question would be d, $100z - xy$. (If you were able to answer it at all without plugging in, you may have forgotten to convert dollars to cents by multiplying z by one hundred.)

If the numbers you choose get too complicated, start over with different numbers. Avoid using 0 or 1 or anything that results in 0 or 1, and cross out the phrase "in terms of x" or "in terms of s and t."

Solving Backwards

An even simpler way to solve using real numbers applies to questions where the answer choices are all numbers. Instead of making up a formula for solving the question, use trial and error to test the answer choices. The one that works is the right answer. There are just two rules:

1. Underline what the question is asking for.
2. Start with answer choice c.

Try this:

One-fifth of a number is four more than one-sixth of the same number. What is the number?

    a. 80
    b. 90
    c. 100
    d. 120
    e. 150

Underline "What is the number?" Now try c—100. One-fifth of 100 is 20. One-sixth of 100 is 16.6666666. Is 20 four more than 16.666666? No.

Now, what should you try next? You want the numbers to get just a little farther apart, so try a bigger number. 120 divided by five is 24. 120 divided by six is 20. *Bada-boom, bada-bing*—24 is four more than 20.

You can try the others if you like, but d works, so it has to be right.

By starting with c, which is in the middle, you were able to discover that you needed a bigger number, thereby eliminating a and b.

22
Math Basics

Even though the Math section on the SAT doesn't test you on the more difficult math concepts you might be learning in school, they do expect you to know several basic concepts you may have forgotten from grade school and middle school. The basics here aren't difficult math, but the concepts are useful for many of the problems on the SAT. This section does not intend to cover all the math content on the test. However, you will find that many questions are based on these simple concepts:

Negative Numbers

Most of us are much more confident thinking about positive numbers. Negative numbers defy our expectations:

- When you add, you expect the value to increase. Adding a negative makes the value *go down*. $(^-3 + {}^-5 = {}^-8)$

- When you subtract, you expect the value to *decrease*. Subtracting a negative makes the value *go up*. ($^-2 - {}^-7 = 5$)

- If you multiply a positive by a negative, you get a bigger negative number, but if you multiply two negative numbers together, the result is positive. ($^-5 \times 3 = {}^-15$, but $^-5 \times {}^-3 = 15$)

- Similarly, when you divide a positive by a negative, the result is negative, but when you divide two negative numbers, they yield a positive result. ($12 \div {}^-3 = {}^-4$, but $^-12 \div {}^-3 = 4$)

- Finally, when you raise a negative number to a power, if it's an odd power, the result stays negative, but if it's an even power, the result becomes positive. ($^-2^3 = {}^-8$, but $^-2^4 = 16$)

Fractions

Fractions also behave unexpectedly. (By "fractions" we mean numbers between $^-1$ and 1.)

- For positive fractions, as the denominator (the number on the bottom) gets bigger, the value of the fraction gets smaller, and vice versa (as the denominator gets smaller, the value of the fraction gets bigger).

- The above statements get reversed for negative fractions.

- When you multiply by a fraction, the result gets smaller (you're essentially dividing).

- When you divide by a fraction, the result gets *bigger* (you're essentially multiplying).

Exponents

You may have learned exponents more recently, but knowing them well will help you pile up right answers:

- $x^2 + x^3 = x^2 + x^3$. You cannot combine these terms by addition.

- $z^2 \times z^3 = z^5$. If the bases are alike (they're both z), to multiply them, you add the exponents.

- $(z^2)^5 = z^{10}$. When raising a power to another power, multiply the exponents.

- $\frac{z^7}{z^3} = z^4$. When dividing exponents with like bases, subtract the exponents.

- $z^{-3} = \frac{1}{z^3}$. Negative exponents become fractions—the base (z) and the positive value of the exponent (3) go on the bottom of the fraction with 1 on the top.

- $z^{(2/3)}$ = the cube root of z squared. When the exponent is a fraction, the numerator (top number) behaves as a normal exponent, but the denominator (bottom number) becomes a root.

- $27^4 = (3^3)^4 = 3^{12}$. Get to know the perfect squares and cubes. When you find them raised to a power, you can simplify them.

- When the test gives you a number raised to a large power—say, 685—the question will always ask you about the units' (ones') digit of the result. If you try typing 764^{685} into your calculator, the result will be too big for your calculator to handle. But you need only the ones' place. If you keep multiplying 4×4, you'll discover that even powers have a 6 in the ones' place and odd powers have 4 ($4^2 = 16$; $4^3 = 64$; $4^8 = 65,536$; $4^{13} = 67,108,864$). Other such patterns exist.

23
Math Quiz

1. Which of the following numbers has the least (lowest) value?

    a. $\frac{1}{9}$ b. $-\frac{1}{9}$ c. $-\frac{1}{10}$ d. $-.01$

2. Which of the following has the greatest (highest) value?

    a. 1000 b. 1.1×102 c. $\frac{11}{.01}$ d. $\frac{10{,}000}{50}$

3. How many prime numbers are even?

    a. none   b. one   c. two   d. three

4. $f(x) = 2x^2 - 2$. Which of the following is equal to $f(x + 2)$?

    a. $2(x + 3)(x + 1)$ b. $x^2 + 4x + 4$ c. $2x^2 + 8x + 8$ d. $2x^2$

5. Which is equal to $(9^x)^3$?

    a. 27^x b. 9^{x+3} c. 3^{5x} d. $3^{4x} \times 3^{2x}$

6. What will be the area of a circle that is inscribed in a square with a perimeter of eight?

   a. π b. 2π c. 4π d. 16

7. If $\frac{x+y}{7} = 3$, what does $7x + 7y$ equal?

   a. 49   b. 112   c. 147   d. 304

Answers

1. Which of the following numbers has the least (lowest) value?

   a. $\frac{1}{9}$ b. $-\frac{1}{9}$ c. $-\frac{1}{10}$ d. $-.01$

This is a deceptively tricky question that requires you to understand how both negative numbers and fractions behave. To answer it correctly, you would have to know the following:

- -5 is less than -2 (even though 5 is greater than 2).
- $\frac{1}{2}$ is bigger than $\frac{1}{7}$ (because the 2 is smaller so it splits the 1 up into fewer pieces).
- When you put the two statements together $-\frac{1}{2}$ is less than $-\frac{1}{7}$.

The correct answer is b, $-\frac{1}{9}$. Positive one-ninth is bigger than positive one-tenth or positive one-one-hundredth, so negative one-ninth would be less.

2. Which of the following has the greatest (highest) value?

   a. 1,000   b. 1.1×102 c. $\frac{11}{.01}$ d. $\frac{10,000}{50}$

To get this question right, you would have to realize that dividing by one-one-hundredth is the same as multiplying by one hundred (just take the fraction that's in the denominator, flip it, and multiply). The correct answer is c.

3. How many prime numbers are even?

    a. none   b. one   c. two   d. three

Two is the only even number that's prime (all the rest are divisible by 2). The correct answer is b.

4. $f(x) = 2x^2 - 2$. Which of the following is equal to $f(x + 2)$?

    a. $2(x + 3)(x + 1)$ b. $x^2 + 4x + 4$ c. $2x^2 + 8x + 8$ d. $2x^2$

You would have to substitute $x + 2$ in for x, foil it out, subtract 2 from the result, and then factor it again. The right answer is a.

5. Which is equal to $(9^x)^3$?

    a. 27^x b. 9^{x+3} c. 3^{5x} d. $3^{4x} \times 3^{2x}$

If you struggled with this one, review your exponent rules. The right answer is d.

6. What will be the area of a circle that is inscribed in a square with a perimeter of eight?

    a. π b. 2π c. 4π d. 16

If the square has a perimeter of 8, each side is 2. Now picture (or draw) the circle inscribed in that square. The circle's diameter is also 2, so its radius is 1. The area of the circle πr^2 is π—answer a.

7. If $\frac{x+y}{7} = 3$, what does $7x + 7y$ equal?

    a. 49   b. 112   c. 147   d. 304

For this problem, you must first recognize that $x + y$ is 21. Then you must factor a 7 out from the second part of the problem to get $7(x + y)$. 7×21 is 147—answer c.

24

The Basics of Timed Writing

How will you handle the timed essay? First of all, this kind of writing assessment is probably nothing new. How often have school tests asked you questions such as "What lessons does *Macbeth* teach us about ambition?" or "What were the main features of the New Deal?" Even short free writes at the beginning of class are a form of timed writing.

What's particularly challenging on the SAT is that the essay topic is often general and vague ("Bad situations can lead to positive outcomes" or "We often take for granted what is most important in life"). You'll have to come up with a specific view on the idea presented and use specific examples to support your perspective. That the topic is unfamiliar (unlike for school, where you've probably discussed *Macbeth* for weeks) makes writing the essay hard. And you don't have much time. In just twenty-five minutes, you'll have to come up with a clear point of view in response to the essay question and provide strong evidence for your perspective.

To do so, you'll need some good examples that support your thesis. You'll have to know your examples well enough to present them quickly, specifically, and coherently. You'll want to organize your ideas in a clear structure for your reader to follow and devise a brief lead-in and a thesis statement. You'll want to vary your sentence structure, using short and long sentences. You'll need transitions to connect your ideas. You'll want to leave a couple of minutes to proofread what you've written. Oh, and make sure your essay is legible!

How Your Essay Is Scored

The College Board hires hundreds of readers—mostly high school and college English teachers—to read and score the essays. Your essay will be evaluated by two readers. Each will give it a score from 1 to 6 (with 6 being the highest), so your raw score for the essay will be anywhere from 2 to 12. If your two readers' scores differ by more than two points, a third reader will read and score your essay.

These readers are not well paid. They will be bored (from reading hundreds of lousy essays) and will probably rush. Your essay does not have to entertain or inspire them, but if you want to get a good score, it must have a coherent structure, be easy to read, and clearly answer the question.

Your Game Plan

- First, see what's in the fridge. If you want to have a sandwich, you don't decide what to put on it before looking in the fridge and seeing what's available. When you open the test and get the essay topic, don't decide whether to agree or disagree until you've evaluated your options and figured out what examples you know well enough to use as evidence. If you decide you agree first and then try to come up with examples, you may discover that all your best examples disagree.

(Also, keep the fridge well stocked. Prepare a couple of examples that you know a lot about. Look for examples that are already familiar to you. Famous people and events from history are always good, but avoid writing about the civil rights movement, which many students will probably use. Too many essays on the same topic make the readers' eyes glaze over. You might also review various pieces of literature you have studied in high school and come up with a list of some political and social issues that might provide examples to use.)

- Now you need a structure. Devise your body paragraphs first. You'll need at least two of them. The body paragraphs should not just list random examples in no particular order. Come up with a way to link your examples. Often, the best way to do this is to write two body paragraphs on two aspects of the same example. Your introduction and concluding paragraphs should be short—two or three sentences. Your body paragraphs will be longer, so plan them well.

- Come up with a lead-in. A lead-in is a two- or three-sentence opening designed to grab the reader's attention and introduce your point. You might consider using a quotation or a quick story or situation, but you can use anything you like so long as it makes a positive first impression on your reader (and is on topic!). Opening by repeating the essay topic ("I agree with the statement...") makes the reader expect a boring essay.

- Vary your sentence structure. Many students seem to think that the longer and more complicated the sentence, the better. Not true. Your essay should contain at least one or two short sentences: "Gandhi was right." Or "Germany lost." There's a lot of punch in a short, to-the-point sentence.

- Make smooth transitions. As you move from one paragraph to the next, use transitional words and phrases to show the logical links and relationships among the ideas being presented. There are many different transitional words that set up relationships between ideas. Keep in mind some of the most common, such as *furthermore, additionally, consequently, however,* and *at the same time.* (You might also want to consult a good writing manual, which often groups transitional words according to the type of relationship they establish— for example, sequence words, similarity words, result/conclusion words, and contrast/concession words.)

- Don't drift off at the end. Even though your conclusion should be short (two or three sentences are plenty), you still need a conclusion to pull your main ideas together.

- Leave time to proofread. A couple of typos or misspelled

words won't cost you (the readers are instructed, after all, to consider this a "first draft"), but having a couple of minutes at the end to look things over can make a big difference.

The crucial step here is the planning. If you don't brainstorm, consider your options, and create a workable structure, you'll have a hard time writing, and what you end up writing may not be coherent. Take time to save time.

Sample Essay Question

In Jim Collins's book *Good to Great,* he explores why some companies "make the leap" from good to great and others don't. As he explains,

> *Good is the enemy of great.*
> *And that is one of the key reasons why we have so little that becomes great.*
> *We don't have great schools, principally because we have good schools. We don't have great government, principally because we have good government. Few people attain great lives, in large part because it is just so easy to settle for a good life. The vast majority of companies never become great, precisely because the vast majority become quite good—and that is their main problem.*

Assignment: What is your view on the idea that "good is the enemy of great"? Plan and write an essay in which you present your perspective on this idea. Support your argument with examples from your studies, reading, observations, and experiences.

How to Write It

- Go to the fridge. To brainstorm successfully, consider only the first part of the topic, then decide how it jibes with the second half of the prompt. In this case, think of things that are "good" but not "great," and then see whether their "good" status prevents them from becoming "great":

    - The history paper you wrote last weekend
    - Grades in general
    - The Atlanta Braves
    - Various products: Coke, McDonald's, the Gap

- Now look at your list and choose the essay that seems to have the most potential. Any of these ideas has some potential, but let's choose the last one—the Gap.

- Devise a structure. This topic lends itself to an obvious structure: a first body paragraph explaining what's good about the Gap and a second that shows how those same qualities keep it from being great.

- Devise a lead-in: "I love fashion." Or maybe: "I was at the Gap the other day, trying to find a gift for my cousin." The second idea works better because it can lead into: "I searched and searched, but, though there were many nice items, nothing special jumped out at me. I ended up buying her a book instead."

- With the structure and lead-in in place, you're ready to write the essay.

Sample Essay

I was at the Gap the other day, trying to find a gift for my cousin. I searched and searched, but, though there were many nice items, nothing special jumped out at me. I ended up buying her a book instead.

The Gap is a good store. The clothes they sell are well made. You don't have to spend a fortune there to buy something that will look good and last a long time. I particularly enjoy finding bargains on the clearance rack. I once bought a gray-and-rust-colored turtleneck for $6.99, which I've now worn for three years. When people ask me where I got it, no one can believe it came from the Gap.

They can't believe it, however, for a reason. Unfortunately, almost everything you find at the Gap lacks style. Being a huge chain, the Gap designs clothes that almost anyone will want to wear. Though they do a good job, the results can't help lacking pizzazz. What's worse, on the rare occasions when they do come out with something even remotely fashionable, half the school is wearing it on Monday morning.

In hindsight, the Gap was not the place to shop for this gift. In order to please most of the people most of the time, the Gap can only aspire to being good — not great. For this particular gift, I wanted something great.

While you probably prefer to have more than twenty-five minutes to think about and then write an essay, being able to write well under time constraints is a great skill to have. Just think about what newspaper reporters do all the time. And most business writing must be done quickly with little time for revision and feedback. Although the writing process in school allows time for revisions, at work you rarely have the time to create multiple drafts, and your teacher won't be there to provide feedback. Like the essay on the Writing section of the SAT, business letters often have to convey information quickly and convincingly. The skills needed to write a timed essay effectively on the new SAT are the same ones people use all the time at work. Keep this information in mind as you practice writing timed essays.

Parents

It is a wise father that knows his own child.

—William Shakespeare, *The Merchant of Venice*

*Buddha said, "If you are to practice giving to yourself, how much more
so to your parents, wife, and children." Therefore you should know
that to give to yourself is a part of giving. To give to your family is also
giving. Even when you give a particle of dust, you should rejoice in
your own act, because you correctly transmit the merit of all buddhas,
and for the first time practice an act of a bodhisattva.*

—Zen Master Dogen (1200–1253), *Moon in a Dewdrop*

25

Taking Your Parents Down Memory Lane

While your mom and dad won't be with you on that early Saturday morning when you take the SAT, they might get intensely involved in the process of anticipating the test. Parents have a lot of different responses to this event. Some are uninvolved, others are occasionally involved, and some become obsessed with it. Of course, there are all sorts of other possibilities for how your parents will respond, just as there are many different schools of thought on parenting.

Sometimes parental involvement takes the form of frequent and persistent questions about what you are doing to prepare. This event can also lead parents to think back on their own experiences with the SAT. You may find that they are *very* eager to share all of this with you.

If your parents took the SAT, don't be surprised if they still remember the test—even if it's been many years since they took it. They probably also remember their scores. Your taking the SAT can bring back their own experiences, which may or may not have been happy ones. Unfortunately, we tend to hang on to—and even brood over—the experiences that disappoint us. Part of what can make the stakes feel high is that parents—with mostly good intentions—may start to plan their revenge on the test through your performance. Your mom or dad might still be wrestling with closeted skeletons about the SAT. Surprisingly enough, an average SAT score has a lot of power to trouble even the most successful adults.

Then, of course, there are parents who did well on the SAT and expect you to do at least as well. This situation recalls the mother who loved biology and can't understand why her child doesn't like it or how he could be having trouble with a subject that's so much fun *and* so interesting, too.

Part of what you and your parents have to acknowledge is that the SAT is one of the first steps in the college process, and the college process, while a *big* deal for you, is also a *big* deal for your parents (maybe even a *bigger* deal). Sooner than you can imagine, you will be off at college. This freaks your parents out. They love and care for you, and part of how they do that is to *worry* about you. Having taken care of you for a long time, they worry about your leaving the nest. Right now your upcoming departure—although it's not imminent—is another source of anxiety for them.

The college process is a rite of passage. It marks enormous changes for parents and children. It may even be *harder* for parents. Keep in mind that they can still remember you as a baby. They can probably recall your first word and your first steps. They can't believe that you are almost ready for college and that you won't be living at home anymore. In your last year or two at home, they may even become more controlling than they have been before, and the SAT may be one of their focal points.

What you have to recognize is how public this rite of passage is. It's possible that your parents and their friends are talking about the college process as much as you and your friends are. This process, whether you like it or not, becomes a type of public viewing of your accomplishments. You yourself have probably participated in this act. Who hasn't been impressed when someone mentions that his daughter goes to Harvard or Princeton? And what about those awkward moments when you ask where someone goes to college and you haven't heard of the school the person names? You find something lame to say like "That's nice" and hope that this person can't tell you haven't heard of the school. When my (Susan's) friend Kenny was at Haverford, he constantly had to explain to enthusiastic parents and grandparents who gushed at his misunderstood response that he hadn't said "Harvard," and in fact he was going to *Haverford*.

Undoubtedly people will ask you where you are applying, and, come April, the question will become where you got in. And—just imagine—it doesn't end there. Throughout your time in college, people will ask you and your parents where you go. You can try to be discreet about the college process, but the ongoing talk about it is hard to avoid. See how public all of this becomes? Other than moving into an isolated cave in a remote part of Alaska (not a bad idea...far fewer applicants...), what can you do about all of this?

This is another instance when Zen can help. Being in the present doesn't include your parents' SAT memories. Help your parents focus on the present by talking frankly with them about the test and about how you are preparing. Include your parents in your preparation. Ask your parents to quiz you on vocabulary words. Discuss op-ed articles with them. If you are working with a tutor or taking a class, discuss the work with your parents. You and your parents might also agree that you will talk about the SAT and the college process during scheduled times and not every time you see each other. Your parents also have to confront those SAT skeletons lingering in their adolescent closets and separate their issues from yours. Let them know about your anxiety and your plans for managing it *and* the test.

Everyone may have good intentions, but you are working at cross-purposes if anxiety about the test is leading to endless arguments, especially the ones in which you end up shouting, "It's my life," and your parents respond with, "When I was a kid, I never..."

26

Seven Damaging Remarks
Well-Meaning Parents Make

As you consider the role your parents are playing in your college process in general and in your preparation for the SAT in particular, remind yourself that they genuinely *do* mean well.

Unfortunately, things often get twisted up around the SAT, and their good intentions can morph into one or more of the following remarks:

1. "There's always community college! Ha, ha, ha..."

You'd be surprised how many parents make nervous jokes like this. We've even heard particularly anxious parents make the comment without joking. A parent making this type of comment—either joking or serious—is playing out the worst-case scenario. When a situation feels out of control, many of us try to manage it by thinking of the absolute worst thing we imagine can happen. Expressing the fear is a way of inoculating ourselves against it. More often than not, unfortunately, this particular joke backfires by linking up with and expressing a student's biggest fear. With all the pressure and hype around college admissions, it's easy to convince yourself that one little slip can land you at the bottom of the heap.

If your parents make jokes like this one (or express such a notion seriously), try to keep your cool. You may have to show some leadership with your parents. Remind them that there are many college options—not just the Ivy League and community colleges. Reassure them that you are preparing or have prepared to do your best.

2. "Don't worry about it. It's no big deal."

A parent telling a teenage child not to worry about the SAT is like a general telling a soldier not to fear going into battle. It's easy for some parents, who've long since cleared these hurdles, to make light of them. "That test is so stupid. You'll do fine" is another way of saying the same thing: *Your concerns are silly*. Now, in addition to the burdens of dealing with the test itself, you may also feel foolish for being concerned.

Being dismissive of something that deeply affects another person is not a helpful way to make him or her less concerned. The words may be temporarily reassuring, but the implied message is really insulting. Perhaps parents do this because they can't deal with seeing their children feel such acute anxiety and they feel unable to help. When you were little, they could give you a hug and a kiss and make your troubles go away. But the SAT is a challenge they can't solve for you.

3. "What did you get on your practice test?"

The question may seem fair. If you are preparing for your SAT and practicing at it, your parents want to know how it's going. But it's a loaded question. We all want to please our parents. We can't help it. It must be genetic. Even if they act pleased with the results, we may *feel* that they are not or that they shouldn't be. Practice tests are just that—practice. Too much scrutiny of practice results creates anxiety and can limit improvement. Make these points to your parents.

4. "*X* is about as high as you can realistically expect to score."

In an effort to make you less anxious, your parents may try to lower your expectations. Your parents' comments in this area can feel like a lack of faith in you. However, they may not really know what you are capable of doing. You may not even fully know this right now. Their assessment may also sound as if they're saying you're not very bright.

Do understand that they may feel scared. They don't want you to be devastated by your results. They want you to feel good about them. But they may not understand the test or how you can improve on it. Your best bet is to set realistic goals and understand what you will have to do to achieve them. If you can get your parents to understand what you're up against and what you plan to do, you may be able to reassure them.

5. "That's good, but you can do better."

Some parents believe that by withholding their approval they can make you try harder. This sort of behavior may make you perform in the short run. But in the long run, the lack of approval undermines your confidence. No matter what you do, it never feels like it's good enough. Even big achievements feel empty, and your efforts seem less and less rewarding. Ultimately, you will have to find your own way with or without your parents' approval. Parents who withhold their approval make the task of identifying your own values and place in the world more difficult, but don't suppose that these are easy challenges for everyone else. In the end, doing your best on the SAT is something you must do for yourself. Improving your ability to read, think, and focus will increase your confidence dramatically.

6. "I'm paying all this money for..."

Some parents have a tendency to use money and paying for things as a way to try to control their children or as the primary means of being involved. Though it's critical to understand the value of money and appreciate the resources you have, we haven't seen many kids become more motivated to do well on the SAT when their parents constantly remind them of how much their test prep or schooling costs. Some kids even get resentful because they feel their parents show their support only with money rather than by talking with them, listening to them, and being around. Again, you may have to take a leadership role with your parents and make these points to them.

7. "You're just not a good standardized test taker."

This comment is akin to "We're just not good at math in this family." It expresses the idea that doing well on the SAT or in particular subjects is inherited or fated at birth and that doing poorly runs in families. Of course, there are differences in how people do on the SAT (or in math classes), but a parent's promoting the notion that her child just isn't good at standardized tests may be the best way to create a self-fulfilling prophecy and to destroy any motivation to try to do well. We've seen too many students (and even students who originally said that both they and their parents don't do well on standardized tests) make enormous improvements on the SAT to accept this remark. Underscore with your parents the specific things you can do to prepare for the test, and urge them not to underestimate your abilities.

27

The Five Characteristics of Supportive Parents

Your parents' behavior usually won't make or break your SAT results. Supportive behaviors, however, can help almost as much as harmful remarks can hurt. Here are our top five:

1. They separate themselves from their child's failures and accomplishments.

To parents, the whole college process can feel like a public evaluation of their performance as parents. If you don't do well—which could mean anything from getting into a particular college to achieving a certain GPA or SAT score—they sometimes feel that they have failed as parents. This insecurity can further complicate what is already a challenging process for you. However, if they can understand that this is *your show*, they will do a much better job of supporting you.

When you sense that your parents feel okay about things, it's easier for you to take control of this process for yourself. Regardless of their behavior, though, the more you take charge, the more the test is about you. That is not to say you can't get support, but be aware of the difference between talking with your parents about your preparation and having them do everything for you. There are lots of things you can do yourself. Remember that you'll take the test on your own.

2. They get informed about the test.

One sure way for parents to ease their own anxieties about your test is for them to get better informed about the SAT. With all the hype surrounding the SAT, it's easy for grownups to imagine an overwhelmingly difficult test. Just as it's important for you to understand the nature of the test, it helps for your parents to do the same. Knowing what you're up against can help the adults in your life calm down and understand how to support you through this process.

3. They listen to their child.

When parents get caught up in their own anxieties, they stop hearing and understanding you. Parents who truly listen provide an invaluable gift.

Parents who listen understand what's going on in your academic life in a meaningful way—not just the grades, but the content you're learning, too. When it comes time to prepare for the SAT, they understand what you're up against because they hear what you have to say about it. Instead of allowing their fears to get the best of them, they let you demystify the test for them.

4. They are available when needed.

When called on, parents can play a key role in your preparation. They can quiz you on vocabulary. They can help you raise your reading level by discussing op-ed articles with you. They can time you on practice tests. The key phrase, however, is *when called on*. Parents who demand to play these roles miss an opportunity to be far more supportive. If they let you call the shots, you will feel empowered and confident.

Parents can also help you deal with the College Board, the company that administers the test. If you have been evaluated and receive accommodations on testing (such as extended time), you will want help in getting all the paperwork in on time and in following up to make sure it gets approved.

5. They genuinely believe in and trust their child's abilities.

This may be a tall order for some parents. All your life, they've had a responsibility to care for you and help you get through difficult situations and challenges. They may like feeling useful—or even indispensable—in your life. And yet the SAT is something you face alone. We've seen how easily students sense parental approval and disapproval. Kids are highly attuned to their parents' comments (whether they appear to be listening or not). Help your parents to understand why they can believe in and trust your abilities. Again, you may have to take a leadership role and fill your parents in on how your preparation is going.

Your Plan

If your mind is calm and constant, you can keep yourself away
from the noisy world even though you are in the midst of it. In the
midst of noise and change, your mind will be quiet and stable.

—Shunryu Suzuki, *Zen Mind, Beginner's Mind*

28
Organization: How's Your Brain's CEO?

Some students struggle with organization. Their backpacks are filled with loose papers, which are mostly torn and wrinkled up. Their textbooks have old handouts and assignments folded up inside them. When a teacher asks them to get out a handout from a week ago, a major paper-shuffling crisis ensues. They can't always find a pencil or pen when they need one. Their friends are tired of being asked to lend a piece of paper whenever a teacher tells the class to take out some.

Big projects terrify these students. They quickly get overwhelmed by details. When a teacher announces a large research project, they feel sick. Of course, many of them are okay when projects get broken down into small parts, but they can't do that themselves. They just don't know where to start.

There are also students who love organization and have

every notebook and folder, from first grade forward, color coded and labeled. They can anticipate the best ways to tackle big projects better than their teachers. These are the students everyone calls for help or the details of homework assignments. They always seem to know the key question to ask in class. Of course, there are also students of all kinds in between these two extremes.

Organization is important for the SAT. Preparing for it is similar to doing a long research project. You have to create a study plan and then break it down into manageable pieces. You also have to stick with it *for weeks*.

Brain research is currently revealing a lot about the area of your brain—sometimes referred to as the brain's CEO by the researchers—that helps you to plan and then stick with your plans. This CEO helps you plan, set priorities, organize thoughts, suppress impulses, anticipate the consequences of your actions, and make shifts (which can help you to respond well to changes or to think flexibly when solving problems).

As you make your SAT study plan, evaluate your brain's CEO—particularly those areas that help you organize for major projects. Think about your habits and figure out a plan that you can manage and that doesn't ask you to become someone you could never be. That is not to say, however, that you won't have to make some changes. You may have to break some of your habits, but strive to set yourself up for success by being realistic about who you are, while simultaneously challenging yourself and making the most of your abilities.

Some of the things to consider:

- How well can you study with friends? If you do your best socializing while supposedly studying, you might not want to study with your best friends. Also, friends can make each other anxious. If you actually do better work when collaborating with others, then put together a study group or sign up for an SAT class. Sometimes those commitments to other people or to a class help us to show up and follow through.

- How well do you take initiative? For example, will you be able to make an SAT study plan on your own? If not, seek the support you need. Don't be embarrassed to ask for help. You might even just need someone to talk to about how anxious you feel. Anxiety can turn us into skillful procrastinators.

- How well do you balance different demands in your life? Does your schedule have time for SAT prep? Think about how much time you have and whether you have to change anything to create time for the SAT.

- How well can you avoid distractions? Figure out *where* and *when* you should study in order to stay focused. Keep in mind that the test is three hours and forty-five minutes long. Build your concentration and focus stamina as you prepare for the SAT. Create study conditions that are quiet and free from distractions. For example, try not to break your concentration every ten minutes by checking e-mail or taking a phone call. You might turn off your computer and your phone when you study. You can then reward yourself by turning them back on when you're done. When you find yourself struggling to stay focused, use the breathing and meditation exercises and strive to clear your mind and get refocused on the present moment. Then return to your work. If you find yourself reading and rereading and being unable to understand anything, take a break; then come back when your mind is clear. Take time to save time.

29

Just Twenty-five Minutes

It's hard to start an exercise program after watching the Olympics. Sure, you feel inspired—how can you not after watching the world's finest athletes astound you with what the human body, at its fittest, can accomplish and look like? And, of course, swimmers like Michael Phelps, who glide through the water with grace and ease, make it look easy. But moving from the comfort of your couch to the pool or the track—no matter the level of your inspiration or desire to get in shape—is hard. Exercise is hard, even when you are in shape.

Focus on what's directly in front of you when you exercise. Try to avoid pondering Olympic dreams (especially from the couch, where you sit comfortably and imagine what it would be like to have the same body as one of the beach volleyball champions or a track and field star). Be realistic. Identify a manageable challenge. Taking a twenty-five-minute walk may be the best way to start getting in shape. The same is true of preparing for the SAT. Start small and build toward your goals.

What's twenty-five minutes? It's easy to spend twenty-five minutes surfing the Internet. (In fact, it's easy for three hours to slip by when you sit down at the computer.) One episode of *The Simpsons* takes about twenty-five minutes. What about a phone call to a friend? Or dinner with your family? The bus ride to school?

Twenty-five minutes is all you need to do one section of a practice SAT. Just start with that. When you do it, commit yourself fully. Turn off the music and the phone. Avoid Instant Messaging; in fact, turn off the computer screen. Just take twenty-five minutes and focus on one section of the test. Live in the moment and give yourself to it. As you do the problems, don't judge your work. Skip and come back. Don't get stuck. Nudge negative ideas away if they surface.

Sometimes getting started is harder than whatever it is you are avoiding. The amount of time and energy that can be spent worrying about getting something done is often greater than the time and energy it would take to tackle the dreaded project. Studying for the SAT is no different, so start small—just twenty-five minutes. And remember, there was a time when even Michael Phelps was dog-paddling.

30

You Can Run a Marathon:
Creating an SAT Study Plan

I (Susan) remember when Oprah ran the Marine Corps Marathon. Sure, her trainer ran every step of it with her, but she still had to run the whole thing herself. Seeing the pictures of her running the marathon made me think that *maybe* I could do one, too. A couple years later, I watched the New York City Marathon. What surprised me most was that the runners came in all shapes and sizes. Some were short and stout, others were tall and thin, and there was pretty much everything else in between. With 30,000 people running the race, there's bound to be a lot of variety. Some of the runners didn't *look* very fit, but they were out there. The runners were all different ages, and some of them even wore costumes. Imagine running a marathon dressed as Gumby! He was there, and he even carried a stuffed Pokey. Now imagine getting passed by Gumby and Pokey. It happened to a friend of mine, who wasn't carrying the weight of a costume!

After I stood on the sidelines of this marathon, I realized that all my assumptions about people who run marathons were wrong. I started to think that *maybe*, just maybe, I could run a marathon myself. I became more confident about doing it when a friend of mine assured me, "Anyone can run a marathon." Of course, he then added the critical qualifier, "If she trains for it."

The same might be true for the SAT: Anyone can do well on the SAT *if* he or she prepares for it. The kind of training program many people pursue for a marathon is not unlike what you need to do for the SAT. Training for a marathon requires consistency and careful building of the athletic skills you will need to run 26.2 miles. You have to understand that running a marathon results from many days of showing up and training. Finishing the marathon—like opening your SAT scores and seeing great results—is a moment of glory. However, behind that moment are days of practice, which are manageable with a good plan.

Before I started my marathon training program, I did a sixteen-week aerobic base-building program. In essence, I went from not running at all to building the base I needed to train for the marathon. By the end of the first program, I was able to run ten miles. It was shocking and exhilarating to complete that first ten-mile run. From there, I began another sixteen-week program in which I built to the 26.2 miles of the marathon. I ran about four times a week, and I kept a chart of what I had to do and when. Nothing made me happier than checking off each workout after I completed it.

As I got stronger and finished longer and longer distances, my confidence grew. Tackling something that seemed impossible changed my understanding of myself and what I am capable of accomplishing. The same can be true for you. As you plan your SAT training program, first figure out how much time you have to prepare. Assess your skills, which you can begin doing by taking a practice SAT test. (You should also use your PSAT scores and the assessments in this book.) In order to have plenty of materials, you should purchase the College Board's *Official SAT Study Guide: For the New SAT*.

There are many different ways to prepare for this test, as you probably already know. Some students go it on their own, using some of the many different published materials that are widely available. Others take test prep classes, and some students work one on one with private tutors. Some schools offer test prep programs for students, which usually take the form of classes, or test prep happens within such classes as English and math. What's important to realize is that you don't have to take an expensive course in order to prepare for the test and do well on it. This book, along with the College Board's book, which has eight practice tests, provides all the materials you will need. Of course, what's essential is *sticking* to whatever program you put together.

The following stories about three different students and their experiences with the SAT illustrate the challenges that many students have faced, as well as ways to manage them. These students will seem like real people, but they aren't based on three particular students. They were created from our experiences working with many different students over the years.

Meet the Students

Catrina—On Her Own

Catrina likes music (indie rock bands and hip-hop) and fashion. She makes her own clothes and wears what her mom would call too much makeup. Catrina has a way of looking you straight in the eye, even when her head is tilted and turned slightly aside, that lets you know she understands more than you think she does. She put the SAT at the top of a list of things she had to do that are "obviously really, really stupid." Her engineer father can still figure out her physics homework and often seems to be a little annoyed with Catrina. She's not quite quick enough for him. (He aced the SAT when he was in high school, by the way.) Her teacher mother, while generally supportive, says Catrina "has no follow-through." Catrina goes to a large public high school in a suburb in Michigan, and she gets good grades, mostly B's and B-pluses, with an occasional A when she likes the teacher.

Catrina's first choice for college was New York University, which she knew was probably a long shot. At worst, she figured that with her grades she'd get into the University of Michigan.

Like many students, Catrina was disappointed by her PSAT scores. She got a 61 in Writing, but only 55 in Reading and 48 in Math (put a zero on the end of each score to get the equivalent

SAT score). At first, Catrina wanted to prepare for the SAT on her own. She didn't think another boring class would do any good. Her mom bought her a workbook, and though she opened it once or twice, she quickly felt nauseated by all the boring-looking exercises. So the book sat on a back corner of her desk and *constantly* reminded her of what she wasn't doing. She and her parents got into lots of arguments about when she was going to study, and though Catrina kept promising she would start, she never did. In the spring, she took the SAT, and her overall score actually went down from her PSAT score. She got 490 on the Math and 580 on the Critical Reading, but a low score on her essay brought the Writing down to a 540. Her combined 1610 was nowhere near high enough for the colleges she hoped to get into. NYU was definitely not an option, and Michigan wasn't looking good either.

The summer before her senior year, Catrina wanted to have an internship in Detroit at a small record company. Her parents struck a deal with her. She got to do the internship, but she also had to take an SAT prep course, which met for ten weeks.

In the course, offered by a large, national test-prep company, Catrina learned to plug in real numbers instead of answering math questions algebraically. She practiced structuring and writing essays and learned to skim the reading passages. Although the strategies helped, the overall experience of the class confirmed Catrina's suspicion that she just wasn't very good at taking standardized tests. She kept making careless errors. Several of the other kids in the class were friends she knew from school, and two of them in particular always seemed to know the right answer long before Catrina even had a clue. Still, Catrina was determined. She worked hard, took extra practice tests, and improved. In the fall, she scored 610 on Writing, 570 on Reading, and 540 on Math—for a new total of 1720. Catrina didn't feel great about the results, but her parents were proud of her efforts. "It's the best you could do," said her dad. Catrina rolled her eyes.

Catrina—Our Way

Our approach would have made much more of Catrina's opportunity to do well. We would have challenged her to stop labeling herself and to take responsibility for the way she reads and understands the questions. A better course of preparation would have revealed to Catrina that almost all her difficulties on the test and many of her difficulties in school result from the jumpy way she reads. Catrina would have learned to expect less from her first reading of the question, to trust her ability to reread (and to make sure that she did reread), and to eliminate downtime spent staring blankly in frustration and anger at the problems. She would have noticed the negative messages she had internalized, would have seen how her jumpy reading style had validated them, and would have realized how mistaken they were. Through careful work on her reading skills, done in part through the op-ed exercise, she would have become a much more consistently strong reader. Of course, she would have also come away with a much higher score and would have become far more confident about her abilities in general.

Trevor—On His Own

Trevor loves baseball and football. He's a high school football player with an outside chance of making a Division III college team. If you ask him, Trev will tell you that he wants to be a general manager or sports agent someday. He doesn't read much. He'd rather watch TV. He gets B's and C's in school, which he admits he'd like to improve. His much older half-siblings from his dad's first marriage went to top colleges (Yale and Stanford) and are currently in graduate school. Trev's parents are divorced, so he lives with his mom and spends every other weekend at his dad's. He goes to a small, warm, and diverse public charter school in Los Angeles. Trev loves to argue and has an opinion about everything. His friends say that he is "smart but not book smart."

Although many of the kids at Trev's school take SAT classes, Trev never followed through with signing up for any of them. His parents told him just to do his best, but his low PSAT scores (38 in Reading, 44 on the Math, and 40 in Writing) worried everyone. His older half-brother, David, who was completing a Ph.D. in economics at UCLA, offered to help. They met at a café in Westwood to come up with a plan for Trevor that involved learning vocabulary and taking practice tests. Trevor was supposed to check in with David every week or two. He never did.

Trevor had a lot of trouble with the vocabulary list. Every time he picked it up to study, the words all just seemed to swim together on the page. He felt ashamed to call David and say that he hadn't done anything. He tried to work on his football, but his fear that his SAT scores might leave him ineligible for college deflated these efforts. David, for his part, felt bad about it, but he was too overwhelmed with grad school to follow up with Trevor.

Trevor forgot to sign up for the SAT in the spring. When he finally took it senior year, he got a 370 in Reading, 480 in Math, and 420 in Writing for a total of 1270.

Trevor—Our Way

Unfortunately, the kid with the biggest needs got the least amount of help. Trevor had a huge hill to climb. Better test preparation would have detected that Trevor had major difficulties with reading. A late reader, Trevor had never learned to decode confidently. Instead he had gotten through by essentially memorizing the shapes of thousands of words. When he came to a big word, he skipped it. This habit made reading painful, so Trevor avoided reading as much as possible. He was so used to this situation that it never occurred to him to ask anyone for help. It's tempting to blame the school, but Trevor was a bright guy. Without meaning to, he effectively hid his struggles with reading. Even at a small school that cares deeply about each student, it's nearly impossible for a teacher with responsibility for serving the needs of a whole class and getting through large chunks of mandated material to notice a well-hidden learning difficulty. All too often, the SAT exposes weaknesses that students have been able to hide in the classroom.

For Trevor to do his best on the SAT, he should have

relearned decoding. Ironically, this probably would not have been very difficult for him. He would have learned to break down big words into syllables, sound out the words, and put them back together again. Then he would have had to reread the sentence to figure out what it meant. Of course, all this takes time. An educational evaluation would have revealed his difficulties and probably would have recommended that he receive extended time on the test.

Our program would have taken this opportunity to engage Trevor's intelligence. We would have challenged Trevor's reading level by having him read op-ed articles every day and would have supported his work with decoding and reading comprehension. Gradually he would have gained confidence. With a kid as bright as Trevor, such a process would have had the potential to produce spectacular results.

Sophia—On Her Own

Sophia works hard. She earns straight A's, but standardized tests are the bane of her existence. No matter how well she does in school, she has never done well on these tests. Her parents are also worried. They met as undergrads at a small college most people have never heard of. Although they are both very successful business people, they constantly rub up against colleagues with degrees from name-brand schools. They believe that they only want the best for their little girl, and they want an Ivy League college. Sophia goes to a highly competitive, all-girls private high school in New York City.

Sophia felt devastated by her PSAT scores: 62 on the Reading, 57 on the Math, and 68 on Writing, for a total of 1870. For many students, these would be outstanding scores, but Sophia knew that coming from a private school in New York City, she would be competing with students who scored at least 2150 or 2200. In her opinion, it just didn't seem fair that her scores were so low, given how hard she worked in school. She often put in more than four hours a night on homework, and she also practiced the piano for at least two hours every day—sometimes even before she left for school in the morning.

Her parents were also worried and concerned about how bad Sophia felt. They started talking to their friends and colleagues and determined that Sophia needed a private tutor for the SAT. They wanted the best possible help for her and didn't mind paying top dollar for a tutor who came highly recommended. It would end up costing them more than $50,000.

At first, Sophia felt encouraged by her tutor. He told her about other students who had achieved huge successes. He assured her that just as she succeeded in school by studying, she could succeed on the SAT in the same way. He met with her twice a week for two hours, and every weekend she took a practice test. It sounded like a lot of work, but Sophia wasn't scared of work. Plus, if it made a difference, it would be worth it.

Sure enough, her practice test scores began to rise. She developed a repertoire of three essays that she could adapt to fit most topics and gained a lot of confidence on the Writing section. Her Reading and Math scores also came up. She began scoring in the high 600s on Reading and even got a 670 on Math once. But then she stopped improving.

Each week her tutor came and went over her mistakes with her. Most of them were silly. He gave her worksheets, and she memorized vocabulary. Sophia began resenting all the time it was taking, but, wanting desperately to succeed, she kept going. They began noticing a pattern on the Math. Sophia would be cruising along until she came to a question somewhere in the middle of the section that she just couldn't get. None of the shortcuts seemed to work. As this pattern continued week after week, she began to expect it and started to lose heart. Her tutor seemed frustrated with her. All she had to do was read the question. The answer was obvious. She agreed, but in the moment it just never seemed to come to her.

Sophia kept plugging away and wound up improving substantially. She felt okay about her 740 on the Writing but only so-so about a 700 on the Reading and ashamed about her 630 on the Math. The combined 2070 meant she would have to readjust her sights for college.

Sophia—Our Way

Sophia would have done much better had she begun by noticing the fundamental way in which the SAT differs from the tests she was used to taking and excelling on at school. Sophia was used to succeeding by studying so hard that she anticipated every question the teacher would ask. On the SAT, such preparation only enhanced Sophia's anxiety when she encountered questions she still didn't know how to do right away. The point on the SAT isn't *to know everything* in advance; it's *to figure things out in the moment.*

Sophia should have focused on how she thinks rather than on the results of practice tests. She placed way too much emphasis on her initial reading of problems. Because Sophia expected to know everything right away, when she read a question and didn't immediately see how to get the right answer, she panicked. She kept trying, but her efforts weren't genuine because she never believed that any new insights would come to her. Instead, she kept going over and over the same old ground, digging in and getting stuck.

Had Sophia learned to skip and come back effectively—to allow her mind to gradually bring the problems that gave her difficulty into clearer focus—she would have become capable of getting almost all the questions right.

Getting-Started Checklist

1. Read *Zen in the Art of the SAT.*

2. Evaluate your PSAT scores and do the reading and anxiety assessments in this book. Use this information as you determine how to prepare for the SAT.

3. Determine how much time you have to prepare and make a specific countdown plan for what you can do between the day you start preparing and the test date. Make a big

calendar with the plan on it. Enjoy checking off items as you get them done.

4. Begin an op-ed reading program (and a more extensive reading program if you have time); aim for reading editorials and op-eds every day.

5. Review the "Some Things You Must Know" chapters and make sure you know them.

6. Purchase and begin doing practice tests in *The Official SAT Study Guide: For the New SAT*.

7. Begin monitoring how you respond to stress; start using the breathing and meditation exercises when you feel anxious.

8. Communicate with your parents about how you are preparing for the SAT. Encourage them to read the "Parents" chapters in this book.

9. Make sure you are acting as the ideal boss and not the demeaning one.

10. Try to see that what may appear to be a crisis may actually be a critical opportunity.

Life Lessons

We want more and still more. Instead of quelling the fire, we reignite it. Instead of seeking inner disarmament — the only kind that counts — we multiply our tools of conquest. And we even forget to check whether the fulfillment of our desire is really the one we had wished for.

—the Dalai Lama

Even the monkey falls from the tree.

—Japanese proverb

31
A Crisis Is a Critical Opportunity

It is as if we change the whole course of life
by changing our attitude towards it.

—Ralph Waldo Emerson

I (Susan) still remember when I first learned that the word *crisis* in Japanese (*kiki*) is defined as "critical opportunity." It was 1987, and I was sitting in my apartment in Carbondale, Colorado, listening to a feature story on Japanese culture on National Public Radio. Although I don't remember the particulars of the story now, I have never forgotten this definition for *crisis*. The reporter went on to explain that we can see the attitude of finding opportunity in what appears to be devastating in how Japan recovered after World War II.

At the time, I was twenty-two years old and had just started my first year of teaching at a rural boarding school. Often the students *and* my colleagues mistook me for a student, and the truth was that I knew little about what I was doing, even if I was officially on the faculty. There were many little crises every day, and I rarely got much sleep as I struggled to prepare for and teach my classes, work in the admissions office, and run a girls' dorm.

When I heard this story on the radio, I remember writing down "crisis = critical opportunity" in my journal and then thinking about it whenever exhaustion and anxiety threatened to overwhelm me. I tried to find possibilities in the challenges I faced. (That is not to say that there weren't many moments when all I wanted to do was sleep or run away.)

I did become good at my job, and I learned a lot about myself as I moved from being a college student to becoming the teacher who had to lead classes rather than sitting comfortably as someone else did. I still think about how to turn a crisis into a critical opportunity whenever life sends me challenges or disappointments.

The SAT may seem like one of the biggest challenges—or crises—you have to face. One of our main goals in writing this book was to show students where the opportunities are in preparing for and taking the SAT. If you become a better reader through preparing for the SAT, then you have taken advantage of the opportunity. If you become more confident about your abilities, then you have taken advantage of another opportunity. If you learn how to manage anxiety and how to focus and concentrate better, then you have taken advantage of even more of the opportunities available.

What's crucial to remember is that all of these skills are important well beyond the SAT. So many of the things you will go on to do will require excellent reading and writing skills, confidence, focus, and concentration. And, of course, these are the skills you need to succeed in college. As you think about how to find the opportunities in the SAT, consider what Emerson noted so long ago. Perhaps he was right: we can change the whole course of our lives by changing our attitude.

32

Feelings Are First, but the Mind Leads

I (Matt) remember watching my wife react to an SAT question. I was trying to explain the nature of the test to her by having her do a problem. From the moment she read the problem, which was a typical SAT math question about integers and multiples and fractions, her emotions took the wheel. To this day, she recalls how the question plunged her back into the darkness of tenth grade math. She had always struggled with math. Like Pavlov's dogs who had been trained to salivate at the sound of a bell even when there wasn't any meal waiting, seeing the words *integer, multiple,* and *fraction* made her panic.

Her reaction was natural enough. We can't control our emotions. They exist in us the way salt exists in the ocean. Just as efforts to turn salt water into fresh water have always proven too costly, so have efforts to control or eliminate emotions. Stifling your feelings may appear to work at first, but there's a steep price: you are training yourself to feel less. Since emotions are the way we experience the world, the more we control them, the more distant the world becomes. Stifled emotions tend to build up and rot inside us, leaving a dull, lingering bitterness that can be difficult to shed.

But emotions get attached to all sorts of things, and, although it's unhealthy to ignore them, it's also unwise to let them run your life. Feelings are sometimes wrong. You may *feel* as if you're going to die when your team loses. You won't. You may *feel* like a worthless nothing when someone you like doesn't like you back. You're not. You may *feel* as if the SAT is impossible for you. It isn't. You can do it—if you will let your mind lead.

"I don't want to do this," said my wife. "I'm terrible at math." But I had known her for several years and had noticed a stubborn determination to master the world of numbers. If we went out to eat, she always wanted to calculate the tip in her head, and she was the one who insisted on balancing the checkbook without a calculator. Whatever her unpleasant experiences in school math had been, her actual ability to do math was fine.

"Just read the problem," I said. "Take it one word at a time."

I knew she could do the problem, but her feelings were running the show. The clamor from her emotional experience was drowning out her mind's abilities to read and to do basic math. Too often in these types of situations, all we notice are our feelings. But when our feelings are the most stirred up, that's when we most need our minds to step in and take charge.

The mind leads. Our minds are capable of taking charge of

even the most extreme situations. We live from our feelings, but they don't have to control our actions. The mind can step up and lead in any direction we choose.

The SAT offers an ideal environment to test this principle. For many of us, taking this test carries tremendous emotional baggage. No matter how many times I go in to take the SAT, the very sight of those answer sheets with all the bubbles makes my skin crawl. I feel anxious and stupid without having even read a single question.

But I know that no matter how strong my feelings are the outcome of the test depends on what my mind does. Will I read the questions accurately? Will my mind process what I read? Will I think through questions methodically without getting frustrated? Will I skip and come back to difficult questions or will I get stuck and frustrated when I don't see how to solve a tricky question right away? When I revisit the questions I've skipped, will I approach them as a beginner with an open mind or as an expert, expecting to know the answer?

One way the mind can lead is through breathing. "Take a deep breath" has become a cliché in our society, but it works. Anxiety causes our breathing to become rapid and shallow. But your mind can take control of your breath. Forcing yourself to take slow, deep breaths can alter how you experience the test. Breathing is the one bodily function you can do both consciously and unconsciously. Be mindful of when you unconsciously begin to breathe rapidly as a response to stress and let your conscious mind change that. Breathing deeply and slowly will reduce your anxiety.

Your mind can also bring your focus back to the present moment—back to the words on the page in front of you, both the ones you understand and the ones you don't. Your mind can insist that you skip a confusing question before wasting time or becoming frustrated. Your mind can bring you back to that same question as a beginner, ready to see it again with new eyes and notice what you may have missed the first time through.

As my wife broke the problem down word by word, she began to see how the pieces fit together. To her surprise, she figured it out and got the right answer.

33
Beginner's Mind (Reprise)

When I (Susan) started taking cello lessons at thirty-nine years old, I realized that learning to play the cello is both humbling and inspiring. Just getting the cello out of the house without bumping it into anything is challenging. It's also not so easy to get it into the case. What stands out, though, is that even when one day I can get a rich sound out of my cello, I will still focus on the same things: how I sit on the edge of my chair and hold the cello, how I hold the bow and round my knuckles as I relax my fingers, how I use my left hand on the fingerboard and round these fingers and apply just the right amount of pressure to hold down the strings.

Every day, when I sit down to play, I will focus on the same things, and each day presents another chance to try again. Each day I need "beginner's mind" to approach the cello and to keep my mind empty, ready, and open to everything. I have to stop imagining myself playing something other than "Twinkle, Twinkle, Little Star" and just focus on the note in "Twinkle" that's right in front of me. It's easy to wander into images of myself playing beautifully for an audience of family and friends who find themselves moved to tears by my music. What I have to remember is that I must always be a beginner—free of self-centered thoughts and unlimited because I am not too demanding or too critical or too eager for others' approval.

Frequently, as I am learning to play, my teacher tells me to breathe and relax. Her instructions make me focus on what is most basic and most essential for playing the cello. She says the cello should become part of my body and the bow should become an extension of my arm. Every time I sit down to play, I try to remember to breathe and relax. Sometimes I remember to do so only because my body has become so tense that my back hurts and my bow hand aches.

The same can happen during tests (or with anything that makes us tense). That's when we most need to slow down, breathe, relax, and return to beginner's mind—the mind that is open, ready, and empty. Keep yourself focused on the present moment; be attentive to the situation at hand and quiet the clamoring thoughts in your mind.

While you will need beginner's mind for the SAT, you will also need it for the rest of your life. As you prepare for the SAT and as you navigate other formidable challenges, remember Shunryu Suzuki's words: "In the beginner's mind there are many possibilities, but in the expert's there are few." Beginner's mind is what allows us to experience life anew each day and to find the beauty and the possibilities in everything, even that which is familiar and that which makes us anxious and uncomfortable.

34
The Myth of Genius (and Stupidity)

Have you ever felt like a genius? Be honest. No one needs to know. Maybe there were those moments when you envisioned yourself debating the president, or accepting your Academy Award, or discovering a cure for cancer, or jumping onstage with your electric guitar to the roar of a stadium full of crazed fans. The details may be a little fuzzy, but you knew in your gut—if only for a brief instant—that you *could* do it, if...

Have you ever felt like a moron? Think of moments when everyone else seemed to get something that you didn't. They made it seem so easy, and yet you couldn't catch on. What was wrong with you? You felt so hopeless. Are you a genius or a moron? You're probably thinking, "Well, I'm neither..." But what if you're both?

About a hundred years ago, a young man in Switzerland had a boring job. When we're bored, we all try to find something to occupy our minds. We go online or read a book or watch TV or play a video game. We daydream about things we want or brood over things that bother us. Some people plan, organize, or cook, and a few people even meditate. But this guy was different.

This guy had to sit at his desk and look busy. He couldn't read a book, and TV, video games, and the Internet had yet to be even imagined. In fact, all three owe their existence at least in part to what this fellow did to pass the time.

Before landing his boring job, he had been in school studying physics. He hadn't done so well in school (which is why he had needed to take this job that bored him), but he loved his subject. So when he had hours and hours to kill, he used the time to think about physics.

He liked to make up thought experiments—little puzzles he would try to solve in his head. He thought about such things as "If you're traveling away from a clock at the speed of light, will you see the hands of the clock move?" He didn't have answers to these questions, but every day he came into work and he had nothing better to do, so he thought about them some more. For years.

As it turns out, we're all lucky that this guy, whose name was Albert Einstein, found his job so boring and loved thinking so much. Very early one morning, he woke up, his head swimming with answers to many of his questions. He hurriedly jotted down notes. After Einstein had spent years playfully noodling during work, his insights were so profound that they would change the way we understand everything in the universe. During the next six weeks he wrote up four of the five theories that would make his career and change the world.

About thirty years later, a young Columbia University student named Harry Rosenfield, who would later go on to become the scholar and public servant who coined the phrase *baby boom*, was sent by a professor to go pick up Einstein, the world's most famous genius, at his home in Princeton, New Jersey, and drive him into the city for a fundraiser. I (Matt) heard this story about a dozen times growing up, as Harry was a good friend of my parents.

It was a cold, rainy night, and when young Harry reached Einstein's house, the brilliant physicist was in a screaming match with his housekeeper about socks. He was refusing to wear any. To Harry's surprise, the great man was also refusing to put on a coat or a hat.

"But, Professor Einstein," pleaded young Harry, "it's cold and raining outside."

"My point exactly," snapped Einstein.

"I can't take you without at least a coat and hat." Harry stood his ground—a little embarrassed. "It's a two-hour drive, sir, and my car has no heat."

"I have a theory," insisted Einstein. He went on to explain that in cold, wet weather, he never wears a hat or scarf or coat or socks because they only get wet.

"But if you don't wear a hat, then your hair gets wet," argued Harry.

"Hair dries" was the nonsensical response. Einstein's point

was that wet outerwear stayed wet against your skin and caused colds—a common belief that had already been proven wrong many times over. Harry didn't dare point out the obvious—that wool, the fabric from which Einstein's coat and hat were made, was famous the world over for keeping people warm, even when wet, and that, in any case, being wet doesn't cause colds: germs cause colds.

"I'm sorry, Professor," he said instead. "I won't be able to take you to New York without at least a coat and hat. I can't be responsible for getting you sick."

Einstein really needed to be at the fundraiser; he was the keynote speaker. So when he saw that Harry wouldn't give in, he finally agreed to dress for the weather.

Was Einstein not smart enough to understand that germs—not a wet head—cause disease? Yes. Yet the same man through a combination of passion and concentration discovered a view of the universe so brilliant and complex that most people (including us) still barely comprehend it.

Being human automatically qualifies you for membership in both clubs: moron and genius. There is no human who is incapable of brilliance, and even the most brilliant among us sometimes acts and feels like a fool. It's the human condition.

Perhaps you're thinking, "But I've never done anything brilliant—what qualifies me as a genius?" Remember what made Einstein succeed: a passion for his subject and relentless concentration. Was Einstein innately more intelligent than other people? Maybe. Did the emphasis his family placed on education and learning make him smarter? Probably—at least in certain ways. But without the repeated focus he brought to his thought experiments, Einstein would have never come up with his Theory of Relativity. He would have just been some guy standing in the rain with no hat on.

What if none of us is a genius and none of us is a moron? What if we're all just thinkers?

The original purpose of the SAT was to identify poor kids who, despite their lousy schools, had the natural smarts to be successful at Harvard. Experience has taught us, however, that instead of revealing everyone's innate intelligence, the SAT offers an opportunity for students to sharpen and improve on the smarts they received at birth.

The difference between you and Einstein is smaller than you think. We have yet to meet a truly stupid student. We've seen plenty of students who had difficulty with reading, but even the weakest readers have been smart in some way. If the scale for intelligence reached from the floor to the ceiling, with a monkey at the floor and Einstein at the ceiling, we would all be somewhere within two inches of the ceiling. We're all humans, and human beings are, by definition, extremely intelligent. How we use that gift is up to us.

Recommended Reading List

As we have often stated, the SAT is fundamentally a reading test; therefore, one of the best ways to prepare is to improve your reading skills and your vocabulary. Below are newspapers, magazines, and books that we recommend. Of course, this list is just a beginning. Ask your school librarian and your teachers for other suggestions.

In order to improve your vocabulary as you read, you have to learn the words you don't know! You probably won't learn them just by seeing them in context. Go a step further and make flash cards for unfamiliar words. Use a good dictionary such as *The American Heritage Dictionary* to find their definitions. Then review your flash cards until you know the words well.

Newspapers
The Los Angeles Times
The New York Times

The Wall Street Journal
The Washington Post

You will find editorials and op-eds in all of them. There are also other types of articles that provide good, challenging reading. Many libraries subscribe to these newspapers.

Magazines

The Atlantic
The Economist
Harper's Magazine
The New Yorker

These are also available in many libraries.

Nonfiction

The Elements of Style, **William Strunk Jr. and E. B. White**
In very few pages, this classic text will teach you about usage, composition, and writing style. And this is the same E. B. White who wrote such children's classics as *Charlotte's Web* and *Stuart Little*.

Fast Food Nation, **Eric Schlosser**
An exposé of the fast food industry.

Into Thin Air, **Jon Krakauer**
A page-turner about the now famous ill-fated Everest expedition.

King of the World, **David Remnick**
A well-written and engaging biography of Muhammad Ali.

A Mind at a Time, Mel Levine
Learn more about learning from one of the country's leading learning specialists.

Moneyball: The Art of Winning an Unfair Game, Michael Lewis
How Billy Beane and the Oakland A's revolutionized baseball.

The Primal Teen: What the New Discoveries About the Teenage Brain Tell Us About Our Kids, Barbara Strauch
The subtitle pretty much says it all.

Also look for anthologies of short nonfiction pieces such as *Progressions: Readings for Writers*, editor Betsy Hilbert; *In Short: A Collection of Brief Creative Nonfiction*, editors Judith Kitchen and Mary Paumier Jones; *The Norton Reader: An Anthology of Expository Prose* 10th ed., editors Linda H. Peterson, John C. Brereton, and Joan E. Hartman; and *The Best American Essays of the Century*, editors Joyce Carol Oates and Robert Atwan.

(These anthologies are fairly expensive, so you might check for them in the library.)

Fiction
There are *hundreds* of possibilities in this category, but here are some books we think you may enjoy and that can get you started. Some of them were written in the nineteenth and early-twentieth centuries, and others were written recently. To learn more about any of them, go to amazon.com or barnesandnoble.com and read the summaries and reviews.

The Amazing Adventures of Kavalier and Clay, **Michael Chabon**
A piece of historical fiction that explores the artists who developed some of the first comic book superheroes.

Animal Farm, **George Orwell**
Orwell's famous satire of the Russian Revolution uses pigs and various other farm animals to illustrate how quickly and brutally those with power become corrupt.

Atonement, **Ian McEwan**
Set before and during World War II, the novel explores the devastating consequences of a young girl's lie.

Frankenstein, **Mary Shelley**
The story of young Victor Frankenstein and his monstrous creation.

Fugitive Pieces, **Anne Michaels**
The fictitious story of Jacob Beer, a Holocaust survivor who is rescued by a Greek geologist in 1940 war-torn Poland.

Great Expectations, **Charles Dickens** (or any novel by Dickens)
The story of Pip, a humble orphan, who dreams of becoming a gentleman.

The Great Gatsby, **F. Scott Fitzgerald**
The story of Jay Gatsby's rise from rags to riches and his quest to win the love of Daisy Buchanan.

Interpreter of Maladies, Jhumpa Lahiri
A collection of beautiful short stories that explore the influences
of culture and tradition on identity and relationships.

Jane Eyre, Charlotte Brontë
Popular since first published in 1847, the novel follows
Jane's early days as an abused orphan and her growth into
a determined and dignified young woman.

Pride and Prejudice, Jane Austen (or any novel by Jane Austen)
Set in a world where young women's best prospects came from
whom they could marry, *Pride and Prejudice* revolves around
the beautiful, proud, and witty Elizabeth Bennett, who doesn't
exactly play the game but still wins it.

Sophie's World: A Novel About the History of Philosophy,
Jostein Gaarder
The subtitle captures the essence of this novel, in which you
will learn Western philosophy by following Sophie's epistolary
journey through it.

The Sun Also Rises, Ernest Hemingway
Hemingway's first big novel explores post–World War I angst by
presenting the stories of various English and American expatri-
ates, who are living in Paris but are traveling together to Spain.

Wuthering Heights, Emily Brontë
A rich and tortured love story set on the lonely moors of
northern England.

If You Want to Learn More About Zen

There are many books about Zen, but we found the ones below particularly appealing and accessible.

Wherever You Go, There You Are, Jon Kabat-Zinn
Zen in the Art of Archery, Eugen Herrigel
Zen Mind, Beginner's Mind, Shunryu Suzuki

If You Want to Learn More About Breathing

Breathing: The Master Key to Self Healing, Andrew Weil, M.D.
(audio CD)

Vocabulary

This list can get you started. Make flash cards for the words and whenever you have a little time, go through them. The definitions here are *brief;* use a good dictionary to enhance them. The dictionary will also show you how each word is pronounced. Additionally, try to find examples of how the words are used, and start using them when you write and speak!

abrasive *adj.* harsh and rough in manner

abstemious *adj.* moderate; avoiding extremes, especially pertaining to food and drink

accolade *n.* praise

acquiesce *vb.* to give in to; consent

aesthetic *adj.* relating to beauty or art

affable *adj.* agreeable

affluent *adj.* wealthy

alacrity *n.* cheerful readiness

ambivalent *adj.* having opposing feelings

ameliorate *vb.* to improve

amenable *adj.* agreeable; willing

amicable *adj.* friendly; agreeable

apathy *n.* lack of emotion; indifference

aperture *n.* an opening

appease *vb.* 1. to calm down; 2. to satisfy

ascetic 1. *adj.* characterized by extreme self-denial;
2. *n.* one who does not allow himself any bodily
pleasures

assuage *vb.* to ease (as in grief) or to satisfy
(as in hunger)

audacity *n.* boldness; nerve

augment *vb.* to increase

auspicious *adj.* favorable; promising

avarice *n.* greed

---

aviary *n.* where birds are kept

balm *n.* soothing ointment

bard *n.* a poet

belligerent *adj.* hostile; argumentative

benevolent *adj.* kind; generous

benign *adj.* kind; harmless

brusque *adj.* abrupt to the point of rudeness; curt

cacophonous *adj.* not harmonious; grating, loud-sounding

callow *adj.* immature; naïve; inexperienced

candor *n.* openness; frankness in expression

cantankerous *adj.* hard to deal with; irritating

capricious *adj.* impulsive; unpredictable

carp *vb.* to complain

castigate *vb.* to criticize harshly

caustic *adj.* bitterly sarcastic

celestial *adj.* heavenly

clandestine *adj.* secretive; hidden

cognizant *adj.* aware

concave *adj.* curved inward

conflagration *n.* a large fire

corpulent *adj.* very fat

credulous *adj.* gullible; willing to believe anything

cryptic *adj.* having hidden meaning; mystifying

culpable *adj.* guilty

cursory *adj.* hasty; quick and unfocused

dearth *n.* lack; scarcity

deference *n.* courteous respect

denigrate *vb.* to belittle

derelict 1. *n.* homeless, unemployed person; vagrant;
2. *adj.* run-down; dilapidated; not fulfilling one's
responsibilities

derogatory *adj.* negative; insulting

didactic *adj.* excessively instructive; moralizing

diffident *adj.* reserved; shy

dilatory *adj.* tardy

diligent *adj.* hard-working

discursive *adj.* wandering from point to point; unfocused

divert *vb.* 1. to change the direction of; 2. to entertain in order to distract one's attention

divisive *adj.* creating disunity

dogged *adj.* determined; obstinate

dogmatic *adj.* dictatorial; insisting on one's point of view

eccentric *adj.* offbeat; unusual

eclectic *adj.* diverse; from a variety of sources

edifice *n.* a building; a structure

efficacious *adj.* effective; efficient

effrontery *n.* gall; nerve

egregious *adj.* particularly bad; flagrant

elegiac *adj.* mournful; sad

elucidate *vb.* to clear up; clarify

empirical *adj.* relying on evidence observed through experimentation

enigmatic *adj.* puzzling; mysterious

ephemeral *adj.* fleeting

equivocal *adj.* uncertain; unclear

esoteric *adj.* known only to a select few; obscure

esteem *n.* respect

ethereal *adj.* airy; ghostlike

evanescent *adj.* tending to vanish like vapor

exacerbate *vb.* to aggravate; worsen

exonerate *vb.* to free from blame; vindicate

expedite *vb.* to speed up the process

expiate *vb.* to make up for one's wrongdoing

extricate *vb.* to take out; remove

facile *adj.* extremely easy

fallacy *n.* false idea; erroneous belief

forensic *adj.* relating to debate, public discourse

formidable *adj.* inspiring fear or awe

fortuitous *adj.* lucky; fortunate

fractious *adj.* cranky

frenetic *adj.* frenzied; frantic

frivolous *adj.* silly; inconsequential

frolic *vb.* to run and play merrily

frugal *adj.* economical; sparing

furtive *adj.* sneaky; secretive

garner *vb.* to collect; accumulate

garrulous *adj.* talkative

germane *adj.* relevant; connected to the point

gregarious *adj.* outgoing; friendly; social

hackneyed *adj.* worn-out; cliché; trite

halcyon *adj.* calm and peaceful; prosperous

harbinger *n.* omen; sign of something to come

heterogeneous *adj.* different; diverse

homogeneous *adj.* all the same; uniform

iconoclast *n.* one who breaks rules; rejects convention

illicit *adj.* illegal

immutable *adj.* unchangeable

impassive *adj.* not susceptible to; showing no emotion

impecunious *adj.* without money

incisive *adj.* sharp; very direct

incorporeal *adj.* not of the body; not physical; ghostly

indigenous *adj.* native to an area

indigent *adj.* extremely poor

indomitable *adj.* unconquerable

ineffable *adj.* indescribable; not able to be expressed

innate *adj.* existing since birth

insidious *adj.* menacing; sinister

insipid *adj.* dull; uninteresting

interminable *adj.* without ending

intrepid *adj.* fearless; bold

invective *n.* insult

itinerant *adj.* moving from place to place

jaded *adj.* worn-out; bored; cynical

lackadaisical *adj.* lacking energy and spirit

lampoon *vb.* to make fun of; satirize

languid *adj.* sluggish; lazy

lithe *adj.* flexible; agile; graceful

lucid *adj.* 1. clear; intelligible; 2. sane

malcontent 1. *n.* grouch; 2. *adj.* unhappy; dissatisfied

malevolent *adj.* wicked; evil

malign *vb.* to say bad things about; slander

maverick *n.* a rebel

mendacious *adj.* lying; false; deceitful

meritorious *adj.* praiseworthy

misanthrope *n.* one who hates people

mitigate *vb.* to make less severe

mollify *vb.* to calm

morose *adj.* sullen; depressed

munificent *adj.* generous

nadir *n.* the lowest point

nebulous *adj.* hazy; vague

nostalgic *adj.* longing for the past

notorious *adj.* famous for doing bad things; infamous

obdurate *adj.* stubborn

obstinate *adj.* stubborn

olfactory *adj.* having to do with the sense of smell

opaque *adj.* 1. unable to see through; 2. difficult to understand

ostracize *vb.* to exclude; exile

pedant *n.* one who parades his learning

penury *n.* extreme poverty; destitution

perfunctory *adj.* done mechanically; without attention
or care

peruse *vb.* to read thoroughly, with great attention

philistine *n.* materialist; one seeking material rather than
intellectual or artistic gain

placid *adj.* calm

plaudit *n.* praise

pragmatic *adj.* practical

precocious *adj.* overly mature and intelligent at an early age

proclivity *n.* inclination

prodigal *adj.* wasteful

prodigy *n.* one with extraordinary talent (especially at
a young age)

profane *vb.* to debase or insult that which is holy

profligate *adj.* wasteful; extravagant

prolific *adj.* very productive; fertile

prosaic *adj.* commonplace; straightforward; dull

provincial *adj.* unsophisticated; narrow-minded

prudent *adj.* wisely cautious; judicious

pseudonym *n.* false name; alias

recant *vb.* to take back one's remarks or faith

rescind *vb.* to repeal; take back

reticent *adj.* reserved; not talkative

sage *n.* a wise person

salient *adj.* outstanding; prominent

salubrious *adj.* good for one's health

salutary *adj.* beneficial; promoting health

sanguine *adj.* confident; bold

scrupulous *adj.* moral; careful and exact

secular *adj.* not related to religion; worldly

soporific *adj.* sleep-inducing

stymie *vb.* to block or hinder

sullied *adj.* dirtied; stained

surfeit *n.* an excess

surreptitious *adj.* secretive; sneaky

sycophant *n.* someone who attempts to get ahead by flattering influential people

tacit *adj.* implied; unspoken

taciturn *adj.* not talkative; reticent; reluctant to talk

tactile *adj.* having to do with the sense of touch

temporal *adj.* related to or concerned with time

tenacious *adj.* unyielding

titanic *adj.* very large; very powerful

torpor *n.* sluggishness; lethargy

tractable *adj.* obedient; easy to control

transient *adj.* fleeting; short-lived

transitory *adj.* temporary

trepidation *n.* fear; nervousness

trite *adj.* overused; unoriginal; hackneyed

unwieldy *adj.* bulky; cumbersome; difficult to manage

vehement *adj.* passionate; intense

vicariously *adv.* felt through the experience of another

virtuoso *n.* one who demonstrates much talent in a specific area

virulent *adj.* extremely poisonous; dangerous

vitriolic *adj.* very bitter (as in criticism)

voluble *adj.* talkative

zealous *adj.* extremely enthusiastic

About the Authors

Matt Bardin, founder and president of Veritas Tutors and Test Prep, has been teaching students to take tests for more than fifteen years. He has found that by helping his students understand their own intelligence and the nature of the SAT, he can help them to drastically improve not only their scores, but also their confidence and self-esteem. Before founding Veritas, Matt taught in the New York City public schools and helped with the start-up of the national teacher corps, Teach For America. A graduate of Princeton, Matt also has an MFA in screenwriting from NYU. He discovered many of the methods presented in this book through teaching himself to do the *New York Times* crossword puzzle while riding the subway on his way to tutoring appointments. He lives in Greenwich Village with his wife and two young children.

Susan Fine has taught English for sixteen years to middle and high school students in Los Angeles, Boston, Taipei, New York City, and Carbondale, Colorado. In addition to teaching, she was the head of the English Department at the Collegiate School in New York City. Through her work at the Grow Network, an education company focused on using assessment to improve instruction in large urban school systems, she developed a strong understanding of the American test industry and the instructional uses of standardized test data. While working at Grow as the director of reading, Susan developed and edited materials for teachers and administrators and created learning activities for families. Susan has degrees from Smith, Middlebury, and Harvard and has spent many years thinking about the teaching of reading comprehension to older students and the best ways to help students understand their own learning processes. Currently, when she's not visiting the American Museum of Natural History with her son, Alex, or playing the cello, she's teaching English part-time to seventh-graders and dreaming about other books she wants to write.